# PSALMS FOR ALL SEASONS

# Psalms
# for All Seasons

John F. Craghan

**LITURGICAL PRESS**
Collegeville, Minnesota

www.litpress.org

*Nihil Obstat:* Reverend Robert Harren, *Censor deputatus.*
*Imprimatur:* ✛ Most Reverend John F. Kinney, J.C.D., D.D., Bishop of Saint Cloud, Minnesota. August 8, 2013.

Cover design by Ann Blattner. Illustration: Thinkstock Photos.

| | 5 | 6 | 7 | 8 | 9 |
|---|---|---|---|---|---|

**Library of Congress Cataloging-in-Publication Data**

Craghan, John F.
    Psalms for all seasons / by John F. Craghan. — Revised Edition.
       pages    cm
    Includes bibliographical references and index.
    ISBN 978-0-8146-3826-2 — ISBN 978-0-8146-3973-3 (ebook)
    1. Bible. Psalms—Meditations.   I. Title.

BS1430.54.C73   2013
223'.206—dc23                        2013016083

For
Father David B. Beaudry
who
announces in both word and person that
God is deeply in love with us

# Contents

# Preface

This work is a revision of my 1993 *Psalms for All Seasons* based
on a new translation of the Psalms in the New American Bible, Revised
Edition (NABRE). While not substantially departing from the original,
this present work introduces changes mainly because of the new translation. I am indebted to Ms. Cackie Upchurch of the Little Rock Scripture Study program for her kind invitation to undertake this revision
as well as for her cheerful assistance and constructive suggestions.

After an introductory chapter, I follow a fixed format in analyzing
fifty-five psalms. First, I seek to situate a particular type of psalm within
the context of the twenty-first century. Here I attempt to note the thrust
of the psalms under discussion and their impact on our modern values.
Second, I briefly outline the characteristics of these psalms. Third, I
study each psalm from a literary perspective, noting structure, vocabulary, themes, and overall religious message. Fourth, I try to engage the
psalm as a modern prayer form. As a result, I endeavor to let the psalm
enter our prayer life, both individual and communal. Fifth, I choose
one or two passages from the New Testament to suggest the significance
of the Hebrew Bible/Old Testament for appreciating the New Testa-
ment/Christian Scriptures. Finally, I summarize the theology of the type
of psalm under examination.

This work seeks to blend scholarship and pastoral theology. It is
my conviction that solid biblical scholarship must affect our manner
of studying and praying the Psalms. However, in order to make this
book more accessible to a wider audience, I have not employed foot-
notes and have omitted discussion of technical points. In their place I

have provided some suggestions for further study. It will be all too evident that I am dependent on the work of a host of scholars, in particular Walter Brueggemann and Luis Alonso Schökel, SJ.

I owe a final word of thanks to two very important people in my life. First, to my wife Barbara Lynne I express my ongoing appreciation for her patience, humor, and recommendations during this time of revision. Second, I wish to thank Father David B. Beaudry, the pastor of Holy Spirit parish in Darboy/Kimberly, Wisconsin, for his inspiring communication of the word of God. At the beginning of each liturgy, as we prepare to enter into the spirit of the celebration of the Eucharist, he reminds us, gently but firmly, that God is deeply in love with us. This reminder is not only verbal but also personal. Thus he reflects in his pastoral care the mission of Jesus, namely, to tell us through action the power of Psalm 36:6: "Lord, your mercy [steadfast love] reaches to heaven; / your fidelity, to the clouds." This little work is a small acknowledgment of my gratitude for such generous commitment to the word of God.

John F. Craghan

# Abbreviations for Biblical References

| | | | | |
|---|---|---|---|---|
| 1 Chr | First Chronicles | | 2 Kgs | Second Kings |
| 1 Cor | First Corinthians | | Lam | Lamentations |
| 2 Cor | Second Corinthians | | Lev | Leviticus |
| Deut | Deuteronomy | | Matt | Matthew |
| Eccl | Ecclesiastes | | Mic | Micah |
| Exod | Exodus | | Neh | Nehemiah |
| Ezek | Ezekiel | | Num | Numbers |
| Gen | Genesis | | 1 Pet | First Peter |
| Heb | Hebrews | | Phil | Philippians |
| Hos | Hosea | | Prov | Proverbs |
| Isa | Isaiah | | Ps(s) | Psalm(s) |
| Jas | James | | Rom | Romans |
| Jer | Jeremiah | | 1 Sam | First Samuel |
| Josh | Joshua | | 2 Sam | Second Samuel |
| 1 Kgs | First Kings | | Wis | Wisdom |

# CHAPTER 1

# Prayer, Psalms, Patterns

What is the nature of prayer? What kind of prayer are the Psalms? Can the Psalms reflect the patterns in our lives with their stages of balance, imbalance, and new balance? It is the purpose of this opening chapter to attempt at least partial answers to these enduring questions.

## *The nature of prayer*

Prayer is as urgent a pastoral problem as ever. While we benefit from our technological age, we also suffer from it. We are served up instant information, much of it discouraging, and challenged to swallow it whole. Our news reporters package much of this information, blocking out some items and seasoning the remains with their own views. Our faith communities also assess world, national, and local events, seeking to uncover God's viewpoint and suggesting the proper way of responding. Prayer and the technological age may strike us as incompatible. However, the fact is that they cannot be separated.

Saint Alphonsus de Liguori, the Doctor of Prayer, called prayer the great means of salvation. Although his eighteenth-century world was quite different from ours, his teaching on prayer is as timely as ever. Prayer, both individual and communal, must reply to our information saturation with faith, hope, and charity. Grounded in the Holy One of Israel, we must dare to expect a new world by reacting to the needs of others that

1

are ultimately the needs of our God. Prayer is not a cop-out from the facts of life, not a retreat to never-never land where pain is lulled and anxiety sedated. Prayer is the denial of passive observation and nonparticipation. Prayer is the affirmation of total involvement. We have to respond to our world in either belief or disbelief. We stand at the crossroads and are challenged to decide. The question is to pray or not to pray.

What does prayer do for us? It forces us to interiorize and reflect. It urges us to dismiss the party line and search ever more deeply into the real, the shocking meaning of daily events. Prayer leads us to adopt different stances, depending on the nature of our world and our own predicament. It can express itself in awe and wonder. It can loosen the gravitational pull of our ego to focus on the goodness of our God, fellow humans, and that joint divine-human venture we call love. It can express itself in thanksgiving. It can lead us to acknowledge the radical newness in our lives that clamors to be known in the song of praise. It can express itself in pain and frustration. It can awaken us to our personal problems and the problems of others. It reminds us that we must share these problems in order to find redemption.

Prayer allows us to think the thoughts of God, not of humans. According to Rabbi Abraham Heschel we use language to inform, but we use prayer to partake. Through prayer we become conformed to the image of God's Son who felt the compulsion for seasons of prayer, who was Luke's paragon of prayer, and who prayed the psalms of his people in a new key. The trajectory of prayer is to become selfless, not selfish, to become transfigured, not disfigured. Prayer constrains us to ask, "What is your will?" not "What is the administration's policy?" Prayer is admission into that frightening world where slogans limp and trite phrases self-destruct. To pray is to acknowledge that things can be otherwise and that we do make a difference.

Prayer allows us to brush up against God himself. We are ushered into the presence of One who does not insist on churchy language, who permits, indeed even encourages, us to employ the raw language of pain and the bubbly vocabulary of joy. Prayer means that God can touch our psyche, piercing to the division of joints and marrow (see Heb 4:12). Prayer is not the privilege of the select few, but the absolute necessity of all. Not to brush up against this God is to cease to be in contact with reality. At prayer we are truly ourselves: weeping and rejoicing, praising and cursing, hearing and being heard.

Prayer empowers us to interact with our technological age. At prayer we find the courage to challenge our world, where the temptation always lurks to treat people as things. At prayer we discover the means to listen to the pain of others and offer healing. At prayer we experience the goodness of others and the encouragement to make that goodness known to a larger audience. At prayer we celebrate the reliability of our God and hence derive confidence to undertake new ventures.

## The Psalms

The Psalms (derived from a Greek word meaning a song sung to the accompaniment of a harplike instrument) are prayer. Although it is virtually impossible to pinpoint the authors of these prayers, they remain the prayer book of Israel. In fact, they are a mini-Bible or—to use Martin Luther's expression—the whole gospel in a nutshell. They are the distillation of the encounter of God's people with their Lord, other nations, and themselves over many centuries. They express in prayer form both the successes and the failures of Israel. Actually, the anonymity of the authors is a plus. The Psalms have become Israel's typical experience of prayer, not simply the once and for all compositions of gifted writers.

The Psalms are also our prayer. Since they are part of the Sacred Scriptures, there is a certain bond between Israel's experience and our own. Our task is to find what the texts may mean for us today. Actually, the utter humanity of the Psalms simplifies this task. As prayers, the Psalms deal in typical fashion with basic human problems and situations. They employ common symbols, such as water, light, and space. The prayer of the temple and the synagogue thus becomes the prayer of the church as well. Hence the history of Israel overlaps with the history of the church and our own personal history.

The basis of Israel's prayer—and our prayer as well—is the covenant. Covenant is a relationship in which a moral bond between parties is defined and affirmed. Because the Lord has chosen Israel as his people, both the Lord and Israel have certain obligations. This relationship, however, is never one-on-one but always triangular: the Lord, the community, and the individual. Covenant and hence prayer based on covenant is always a dangerous undertaking. It presumes that the individual can truly interact with God only by including the community.

Even the most personal and intimate prayer of an individual is bound up with the good of the community. Prayer rooted in covenant exposes the shallowness of this sentiment: "God never gets in my way, only humans do!"

The Psalms were principally composed for liturgical worship. They are poetry, not prose. The chief characteristic of Hebrew poetry is parallelism or a rhyming of sense. In synonymous parallelism the second part or stich echoes the first in slightly different language. This second part makes us reexperience the first part by intensifying or specifying. For example, "Why do the nations protest / and the peoples conspire in vain?" (Ps 2:1). In antithetic parallelism the second part opposes the first: "Because the LORD knows the way of the just, / but the way of the wicked leads to ruin" (Ps 1:6). In synthetic parallelism the second part develops or complements the first: "For the LORD is the great God, / the great king over all gods" (Ps 95:3).

In appropriating this poetry for our prayer life, we immediately note that it may jar our regular prayer formulas. In many ways our theological language is very intellectual. We seem to prefer council statements or third-person definitions. We are more at home with "The Almighty in his providence will not allow his creation to miscarry" than with "The LORD is my shepherd; / there is nothing I lack" (Ps 23:1). We are likely to choose "To the Divine Person worship is due" over "Give praise with tambourines and dance, / praise him with strings and pipes. / Give praise with crashing cymbals, / praise him with sounding cymbals" (Ps 150:4-5). From our religious background we talk *about* God, whereas in the Psalms we talk *to* God. The imagery of the Psalms, therefore, as well as the I-You-Community relationship, challenge us to adopt new prayer habits. We are asked to share in the poetic prayer of Israel and thus add our voice to the ongoing chorus of praise and petition.

In praying the Psalms, we encounter our God through the words of the poet. In communicating that experience, the poet chooses images and symbols. It is these images and symbols that speak to our prayer needs. We are to immerse ourselves in that language so that it becomes a springboard for enriching our own particular situations. The poet's description of awe, fear, love, hate, and so forth, becomes ours in a special way when we allow it to touch our world. Indeed it is a worthwhile exercise to attempt to write our own psalms and apply the images and symbols to our daily lives.

## The patterns of human life

Examining the question of adapting the Psalms to our own prayer needs, Walter Brueggemann observes that our human experience is quite variable. We know those moments when balance and harmony are the rule. There are no sudden, devastating shocks or upsetting blows. We enjoy the security that our past has provided. Given that state, we believe that "God's in his heaven, all's right with the world." However, we also know those times when our secure and seemingly indestructible world begins to collapse. The tried-and-true axioms of the past simply will not work. We attempt to rebuild our world but we do it the old-fashioned way. The results are deeper despair and greater disillusionment. Depending on our willingness to let go, we may begin to reach a point where we are willing to admit newness into our lives. This is not a newness built on our own efforts or based on our own premises. It is a newness that comes as gift or grace. If we are willing to run the risk of a world built along new lines, we overcome our discouragement and frustration by reaching for the promise of Another. Though we may regain what we had "before the fall," we are clearly different people. We have experienced the fall and, as a result, our values have shifted. Brueggemann labels these patterns of human life: orientation, disorientation, and reorientation or new orientation.

Brueggemann has suggested that certain types of psalms fit these different stages. Thus there are psalms that speak to our needs, that reflect "where we're at." This book is an effort to range different psalm types according to our (or our community's) place in this pattern of orientation-disorientation-reorientation. Under orientation there are hymns or psalms of descriptive praise (chap. 2), psalms of trust or confidence (chap. 3), wisdom psalms (chap. 4), and certain royal psalms (chap. 5). Under disorientation there are laments, both individual and communal (chap. 6). Finally, under reorientation there are thanksgivings or psalms of declarative praise, again both individual and communal (chap. 7).

A few cautions are in order. First, this orientation-disorientation-reorientation process is not a neat grid that explains the entire book of Psalms. Rather, it seems to be a useful approach for appreciating many of the psalms and adapting them to our prayer life. Second, humans experience cycles in their prayer life, just as in other dimensions of life. If reorientation begins to become the normal state of an individual, then reorientation becomes orientation. Third, we are urged to pray all the psalms. If we choose to focus only on psalms of orientation, we may cease to be aware of people who are reeling from the trauma of disorientation. Hence we may legitimately pray the psalms of disorientation despite our own state of security. Covenant demands such reaching out. Or—to adopt the stance of Paul—"If [one] part suffers, all the parts suffer with it" (1 Cor 12:26).

# CHAPTER 2

# In Praise of Dependence
## The Psalms of Descriptive Praise

### Ancients versus moderns

In the world of the ancient Near East the gods were in charge. They provided that order and security without which human life was judged to be impossible. The deliberations of the gods thus regulated all aspects of the lives of men, women, and children. In turn, humans were called upon to acknowledge this total dependence by singing hymns to their gods. Such hymns articulated in praise form the supreme value of dependence.

In our age autonomy or independence, rather than dependence, is the supreme virtue. Hence praise does not come readily to our lips. Our human tendency is to be locked into ourselves, into our private little world where no one may intrude except to acknowledge our autonomy. We suffer, therefore, from the debilitating disease of egoism.

Even if we manage to admit the centrality of God in our lives, we find it very difficult to grant center stage to other humans. We will confess only one Creator, thereby eliminating all cocreators. We may unshackle ourselves to praise the Creator but we will not, indeed at times cannot, advance to the point of praising the Creator's presence in others. Though ample evidence of the goodness of others and hence the reflection of the Creator surrounds us, we choose to set limits to our God's capacity to be revealed in others.

### Hymns or psalms of descriptive praise

Psalms of descriptive praise, also known as hymns, praise God for his ongoing, regular care of the world and humanity. Hence God is one who characteristically provides and is worthy of praise. In these psalms God continues the work begun in the initial creation.

The structure of the psalms of descriptive praise is relatively simple. In the introduction the psalmist expresses his intention to praise God or invites others to join in the praise. In the main section the psalmist offers reasons or motives for such praise. This section consequently sustains the sense of awe and wonder in God's presence and involves the worshiping community in God's activities. In the conclusion the psalmist usually restates elements found in the introduction.

Since psalms of descriptive praise dwell on God's ongoing care for his creation, they express harmony, stability, and balance. As a result, they clearly exemplify the mindset of orientation with its orderly flow of events. In terms of prayer these psalms challenge us to withstand the self-seeking force of our ego and thus sing the goodness of Another who continues to create—so often in and through others. The more human we become, that is, the more prayerful we become, the more we are open to God and God's goodness in others. To put it negatively, a life without praise is not a human life.

### Psalm 117
### The Nations Called To Praise

¹Praise the LORD, all you nations!
    Extol him, all you peoples!
²His mercy for us is strong;
    the faithfulness of the LORD is forever.
Hallelujah!

This psalm is the shortest in the entire book of Psalms. At the same time, however, it illustrates the whole ministry of descriptive praise. Perhaps using a certain amount of exaggeration, the psalmist calls upon the foreign nations to praise and extol. The motive for such praise is found in the Lord's mercy and faithfulness. According to a footnote to Psalm 5:8 in the NABRE "mercy" may also be rendered "steadfast love" and "loving kindness." "Loyalty" is another possible translation, a loyalty reminiscent of "semper fidelis." According to this psalm the Lord has kept his part of the covenant relationship. What Israel has experienced in dealing with the Lord grounds the invitation to the foreign nations. Such goodness, while it demands acknowledgment on the part of Israelites, also calls for recognition by non-Israelites.

At prayer we have the time and the setting to review the Lord's loyalty both as individuals and as members of the community. Because this God has responded to our problems and needs, we must break out in praise. There is no need to tabulate each particular intervention by our God. Perhaps it is sufficient to recall one category or segment in our lives where the Lord has consistently demonstrated such fidelity.

This psalm may pull us in another direction as well. It may remind us of our need to share the manifestations of God's love with those outside our faith community. This psalm quietly challenges us to be the spokespersons of our God's concern for all humanity. Ultimately this shortest of psalms suggests the universal thrust of our lives, embracing all nations and peoples (see also Rom 15:11).

## Psalm 33
## Praise of God's Power and Providence

I

¹Rejoice, you righteous, in the LORD;
  praise from the upright is fitting.
²Give thanks to the LORD on the harp;
  on the ten-stringed lyre offer praise.
³Sing to him a new song;
  skillfully play with joyful chant.
⁴For the LORD's word is upright;
  all his works are trustworthy.
⁵He loves justice and right.
  The earth is full of the mercy of the LORD.

II

⁶By the LORD's word the heavens were made;
  by the breath of his mouth all their host.
⁷He gathered the waters of the sea as a mound;
  he sets the deep into storage vaults.

III

⁸Let all the earth fear the LORD;
   let all who dwell in the world show him reverence.
⁹For he spoke, and it came to be,
   commanded, and it stood in place.
¹⁰The LORD foils the plan of nations,
   frustrates the designs of peoples.
¹¹But the plan of the LORD stands forever,
   the designs of his heart through all generations.
¹²Blessed is the nation whose God is the LORD,
   the people chosen as his inheritance.

IV

¹³From heaven the LORD looks down
   and observes the children of Adam,
¹⁴From his dwelling place he surveys
   all who dwell on earth.
¹⁵The One who fashioned together their hearts
   is the One who knows all their works.

V

¹⁶A king is not saved by a great army,
   nor a warrior delivered by great strength.
¹⁷Useless is the horse for safety;
   despite its great strength, it cannot be saved.
¹⁸Behold, the eye of the LORD is upon those who fear him,
   upon those who count on his mercy,
¹⁹To deliver their soul from death,
   and to keep them alive through famine.

VI

²⁰Our soul waits for the LORD,
   he is our help and shield.
²¹For in him our hearts rejoice;
   in his holy name we trust.
²²May your mercy, LORD, be upon us;
   as we put our hope in you.

This psalm speaks of God's orderly world in which the divine word brings about creation and continues to sustain it. Its structure is as follows: (1) introduction exhorting Israel to praise the Lord (vv. 1-3);

(2) God's creative word (vv. 4-9); (3) God's supremacy over the entire earth (vv. 10-15); (4) God alone as savior (vv. 16-19); (5) conclusion (vv. 20-22).

The psalmist highlights God's creative word and surveillance. There is no effort involved in creation. God merely speaks and the world comes into existence (vv. 6, 9). However, the psalmist is careful to point out that this Creator is not an absentee landlord. From heaven the Lord surveys the entire human race (vv. 13-15). Nonetheless God singles out Israel as most deserving of his divine vigilance (vv. 18-19). Praise is indeed the appropriate response from God's chosen people.

While the author acknowledges the chasm separating God from humans (v. 8), he also duly notes a certain bond between the Creator and Israel. God rules this world, a world in which he graciously provides but also bids the righteous and upright to acknowledge such generosity (v. 1). Similarly, the Lord's word is true or upright (v. 4) and he loves justice (v. 5). The psalmist implies that genuine human conduct (righteousness, uprightness) goes hand in hand with God's creative and sustaining word. Praise of God's creation is also the acknowledgment of the need for human response in the form of fidelity and commitment to Israel's Lord.

This psalm may help us to realize that our daily lives are the raw material for praise of the Creator. Where love and justice prevail, God's world/our world remains orderly. But where hatred and injustice prevail, God's world/our world becomes chaotic (see Gen 6:11-14). This psalm may also invite us to praise the cocreators who through fidelity and patience continue to make this world what the Creator intended it to be. In offering praise to our God, we are urged to offer praise to such sisters and brothers.

## Psalm 104
## Praise of God the Creator

I

¹Bless the LORD, my soul!
  LORD, my God, you are great indeed!
You are clothed with majesty and splendor,
  ²robed in light as with a cloak.
You spread out the heavens like a tent;
  ³setting the beams of your chambers upon the waters.

You make the clouds your chariot;
    traveling on the wings of the wind.
[4]You make the winds your messengers;
    flaming fire, your ministers.

II

[5]You fixed the earth on its foundation,
    so it can never be shaken.
[6]The deeps covered it like a garment;
    above the mountains stood the waters.
[7]At your rebuke they took flight;
    at the sound of your thunder they fled.
[8]They rushed up the mountains, down the valleys
    to the place you had fixed for them.
[9]You set a limit they cannot pass;
    never again will they cover the earth.

III

[10]You made springs flow in wadies
    that wind among the mountains.
[11]They give drink to every beast of the field;
    here wild asses quench their thirst.
[12]Beside them the birds of heaven nest;
    among the branches they sing.
[13]You water the mountains from your chambers;
    from the fruit of your labor the earth abounds.
[14]You make the grass grow for the cattle
    and plants for people's work
    to bring forth food from the earth,
    [15]wine to gladden their hearts,
    oil to make their faces shine,
    and bread to sustain the human heart.
[16]The trees of the LORD drink their fill,
    the cedars of Lebanon, which you planted.
[17]There the birds build their nests;
    the stork in the junipers, its home.
[18]The high mountains are for wild goats;
    the rocky cliffs, a refuge for badgers.

IV

<sup>19</sup>You made the moon to mark the seasons,
 the sun that knows the hour of its setting.
<sup>20</sup>You bring darkness and night falls,
 then all the animals of the forest wander about.
<sup>21</sup>Young lions roar for prey;
 they seek their food from God.
<sup>22</sup>When the sun rises, they steal away
 and settle down in their dens.
<sup>23</sup>People go out to their work,
 to their labor till evening falls.

V

<sup>24</sup>How varied are your works, LORD!
 In wisdom you have made them all;
 the earth is full of your creatures.
<sup>25</sup>There is the sea, great and wide!
 It teems with countless beings,
 living things both large and small.
<sup>26</sup>There ships ply their course
 and Leviathan, whom you formed to play with.

VI

<sup>27</sup>All of these look to you
 to give them food in due time.
<sup>28</sup>When you give it to them, they gather;
 when you open your hand, they are well filled.
<sup>29</sup>When you hide your face, they panic.
 Take away their breath, they perish
 and return to the dust.
<sup>30</sup>Send forth your spirit, they are created
 and you renew the face of the earth.

VII

<sup>31</sup>May the glory of the LORD endure forever;
 may the LORD be glad in his works!
<sup>32</sup>Who looks at the earth and it trembles,
 touches the mountains and they smoke!
<sup>33</sup>I will sing to the LORD all my life;
 I will sing praise to my God while I live.

<sup>34</sup>May my meditation be pleasing to him;
    I will rejoice in the LORD.
<sup>35</sup>May sinners vanish from the earth,
    and the wicked be no more.
Bless the LORD, my soul! Hallelujah!

This beautiful psalm attests to the symmetry and splendor of God's magnificent creation. The human person (in v. 1 "soul" means the conscious, reflecting self) feels compelled to break out in praise (in v. 1 "bless" means to praise, not make holy). The structure of the psalm may follow these lines: (1) creation of the world (vv. 1-9); (2) provision of water (vv. 10-18); (3) creation of the moon and sun as well as the nightly and daily acquisition of food (vv. 19-26); (4) prayer for rain (vv. 27-35).

The psalm exudes a sense of confidence and ease on God's part. This God is both in charge and in control of creation. The "sea" demonstrates this feeling of serenity. Whereas elsewhere the sea is often a force that God must defeat and subject (see Job 38:8-11), here it is God's plaything (v. 25). Indeed Leviathan, the mythical monster linked to primeval chaos (see Ps 74:14), merely provides God with amusement (v. 26).

The psalm emphasizes the connectedness of all creation. Humans as well as the rest of creation depend on God's providence and frugality for daily needs (vv. 27-28). All living creatures rely on God for their life-breath (v. 29). Life independent of God is utterly unthinkable.

While experience attests to earthquakes (v. 32) and the presence of evil in creation (v. 35), the overwhelming thrust of this psalm is the awareness of splendor and awe. It is such awareness that makes the psalmist break out into a song of praise (vv. 33-34). To refuse to praise God is to deprive oneself of a rightful place in this world. On the other hand, to praise God is to connect oneself with all the beauty in this world.

Reflection on this psalm must raise questions of ecology and our attitude toward the environment. To be sure, this psalmist is an environmentalist. But far from being a catalog or inventory of the world, this psalm is a profound statement of our connectedness with all of creation. Our efforts to care for the environment thus become a song of praise for the God who insists on the orderliness of creation. We are summoned, not to see nature as one more challenge, but to regard it as another voice in the great chorus of praise to God. After all, we must take time to smell the flowers and consciously preserve the delicate balance of creation.

Another aspect of this psalm worthy of our reflection is the mention of humans as workers in God's creation. The psalmist assumes that human labor is not a curse or drudgery, but rather another ingredient in God's overall plan of creation (see Gen 2:5-8). This psalm urges us to see our form of work, no matter what it is, as another way to praise the Creator. To perform our job in such a way that all of creation is served is to appropriate the meaning of praise in this psalm.

## Psalm 8
### Divine Majesty and Human Dignity

> [1]For the leader; "upon the *gittith*." A psalm of David.
> [2]O Lord, our Lord,
>    how awesome is your name through all the earth!
> I will sing of your majesty above the heavens
>    [3]with the mouths of babes and infants.
> You have established a bulwark against your foes,
>    to silence enemy and avenger.
> [4]When I see your heavens, the work of your fingers,
>    the moon and stars that you set in place—
> [5]What is man that you are mindful of him,
>    and a son of man that you care for him?
> [6]Yet you have made him little less than a god,
>    crowned him with glory and honor.
> [7]You have given him rule over the works of your hands,
>    put all things at his feet:
> [8]All sheep and oxen,
>    even the beasts of the field,
> [9]The birds of the air, the fish of the sea,
>    and whatever swims the paths of the seas.
>
> [10]O Lord, our Lord,
>    how awesome is your name through all the earth!

This psalm begins with a superscription, that is, titles or notes that stem from pre-Christian Jewish tradition. (All but thirty-four psalms have such labels.) "For the leader" is not totally clear. It may mean that such psalms were once found in a collection of "the choirmaster." The "gittith" is either a musical instrument or the title of the melody for singing the psalm. "A psalm of David" can mean that David composed the psalm, the psalm was composed in homage to David, or the psalm was placed under the patronage of David.

This psalm opens and closes with the same expression: "O LORD, our Lord, / how awesome is your name through all the earth!" (vv. 1, 10). (When a word, phrase, or poetic line is found in both the opening and closing lines of a psalm or section of a psalm, this repetition is called an *inclusio* or envelope structure.) This repetition creates a climate of contemplation, beckoning to the audience to acknowledge the majesty of the God of Israel in the body of the psalm. However, the psalmist soon interjects a disconcerting question. If contemplation of the heavens with the moon and stars (v. 4) provokes a cry of admiration, then the vision of humans (v. 5) seems to provoke a cry of desperation. Humans occupy a position slightly below a god (v. 6, probably a member of God's heavenly court [see Ps 82:1]). What is involved is the risk of creation.

In verses 2-3 the author sets up a contrast between babes and infants on the one hand and foes, enemy, and avenger on the other. The author next heightens the contrast by dwelling on the royalty of humans. He describes them with the typical qualities of a king in verse 6: crown, glory, and honor. In verses 7-9 the poet develops this royal character by picturing humans after the manner of Genesis 1. Humans, therefore, share in God's own glory so that they may represent him on earth. The God of this psalm is one who can delegate, not hoard power and thereby escape the danger of reducing humans to the level of puppets. However, the contrast of verse 3 still lingers. Which way will humans go with their regal power? Will they be babes and infants or will they be foes, the enemy, and the avenger?

This psalm raises in poetic form the dilemma of the Garden of Eden. Obviously the writer knows that humans have a tendency to renounce their creatureliness and assume the arrogant airs of absolute monarchy. We all like to play God, thereby making ourselves the center of the universe and the absolute norm that determines good and evil. However, the opposite of rebellion is the ministry of praise. The attitude opposed to vengeful rebellion is the attitude of the child. Here we have a world of happiness, discovery, and affirmation. In such a world awe, namely, astonishment at God's accomplishments, reigns supreme. Instead of being rebellious giants, we humans are exhorted to be infants discovering and subsequently praising our God.

To praise God is to acknowledge God's risk in creating. However, to continue to praise is to opt for the status of responsible kings and queens in the typical order of orientation. To praise this God is to realize that we have obligations to this God and this God's creation. This psalm challenges us to be authors of life, not proliferators of death.

## Psalm 19
## God's Glory in the Heavens and in the Law

[1]For the leader. A psalm of David.

I

[2]The heavens declare the glory of God;
    the firmament proclaims the works of his hands.
[3]Day unto day pours forth speech;
    night unto night whispers knowledge.
[4]There is no speech, no words;
    their voice is not heard;
[5]A report goes forth through all the earth,
    their messages, to the ends of the world.
He has pitched in them a tent for the sun;
    [6]it comes forth like a bridegroom from his canopy,
    and like a hero joyfully runs its course.
[7]From one end of the heavens it comes forth;
    its course runs through to the other;
    nothing escapes its heat.

II

[8]The law of the LORD is perfect,
    refreshing the soul.
The decree of the LORD is trustworthy,
    giving wisdom to the simple.
[9]The precepts of the LORD are right,
    rejoicing the heart.
The command of the LORD is clear,
    enlightening the eye.
[10]The fear of the LORD is pure,
    enduring forever.

The statutes of the LORD are true,
      all of them just;
[11]More desirable than gold,
      than a hoard of purest gold,
Sweeter also than honey
      or drippings from the comb.
[12]By them your servant is warned;
      obeying them brings much reward.
III
[13]Who can detect trespasses?
      Cleanse me from my inadvertent sins.
[14]Also from arrogant ones restrain your servant;
      let them never control me.
Then shall I be blameless,
      innocent of grave sin.
[15]Let the words of my mouth be acceptable,
      the thoughts of my heart before you,
      LORD, my rock and my redeemer.

This prayer consists of two distinct but complementary psalms. The first and older psalm comprises verses 2-7; it is a psalm of descriptive praise. The second and younger psalm is verses 8-15 and is basically a wisdom psalm. The beauty of this composition is that the second psalm develops the theme of divine presence by reflecting on God's directives and Israel's traditions.

The first psalm was originally a pagan hymn honoring the Semitic god El (translated "God" in v. 2). The heavenly phenomena, especially the sun, proclaim inaudibly yet realistically the praise of El. In its Israelite form the hymn naturally praises the God of Israel. It is possible that the heavens and the firmament (v. 2) are personified spaces while day and night (v. 3) are personified times. The activity of all four consists in speaking. The earth functions as a great audience hall that listens to the heavenly discourse. Though words are not employed (v. 4), the message reaches to the ends of the earth (v. 5), communicating God's glory and activity (v. 2).

The sun god in the pagan myth had a tent where he spent the night with his beloved and from which he departed in the morning to resume his circuit with renewed vigor and vitality. In its Israelite form the sun does not speak. Instead, it carries along and repeats the message of the heavens and the firmament.

The second psalm, far from destroying the beauty of the first, now takes the theme of God's presence in another direction. It is not only nature that announces in inexpressible speech the divine presence. It is also God's "torah" (translated "law" in v. 8), that is, God's wise instruction, including all of God's directives and Israel's traditions. However, this torah is intelligible language that articulates God's will. Like the sun, God's revelation rejoices the heart and enlightens the eye (v. 9), even to the point of illuminating one's inadvertent faults (v. 13).

In its final form this psalm is not an "either-or" but a "both-and." One does not find God's presence only in nature to the exclusion of revelation or vice versa. Rather, one finds God both in the beauty of nature and in the beauty of the revealed word. The worship in the universe and in the temple should complement each other and lead to mutual appreciation.

At prayer we are invited to listen to the inaudible but real God who commands the works of creation to communicate the depth of his love. After all, this God is our rock (v. 15) and hence the basis of our firm world. He is also our redeemer (v. 15), a family member, often the next of kin, who must rally to the aid of a disadvantaged relative, for example, by buying property to keep it in the family. At prayer we are urged to listen to the ongoing revelation of his concern. In turn, we are challenged to join the chorus of "He is good, very good." We are invited as well to let the revealed word have an impact on our total person ("soul" in v. 8). Ultimately both forms of manifestation contribute to the orderliness of our world. Ours is thereby a world made firm by nature and solidified by the spoken word.

## Psalm 29
## The Lord of Majesty Acclaimed as King of the World

¹A psalm of David.

I

Give to the LORD, you sons of God,
   give to the LORD glory and might;
²Give to the LORD the glory due his name.
   Bow down before the LORD's holy splendor!

II

³The voice of the LORD is over the waters;
   the God of glory thunders,
   the LORD, over the mighty waters.
⁴The voice of the LORD is power;
   the voice of the LORD is splendor.
⁵The voice of the LORD cracks the cedars;
   the LORD splinters the cedars of Lebanon,
⁶Makes Lebanon leap like a calf,
   and Sirion like a young bull.
⁷The voice of the LORD strikes with fiery flame;
   ⁸the voice of the LORD shakes the desert;
   the LORD shakes the desert of Kadesh.
⁹The voice of the LORD makes the deer dance
   and strips the forests bare.
   All in his Temple say, "Glory!"

III

¹⁰The LORD sits enthroned above the flood!
   The LORD reigns as king forever!
¹¹May the LORD give might to his people;
   may the LORD bless his people with peace!

Scholars generally agree that this psalm was originally a pagan composition extolling the Canaanite god Baal, the weather god who through storms and rains brings fertility to the earth. Here the imagery deals with the end of the summer drought and the renewal of life and fertility with the arrival of the fall rains. The heavenly beings in verse 1 were originally the minor gods of the Canaanite pantheon. In appropriating this hymn for worship, Israel substituted the name of Yahweh (translated as "the LORD") for that of Baal. Hence the Lord is acknowledged as the cosmic lord who meets the fertility needs of his people. This psalm is a perfect example of the movement of orientation, praising the Lord's recurring goodness in the form of rain.

After the introduction (vv. 1-2), the poet tries to create in the main section (vv. 3-9) a mighty tempest as a manifestation of God and especially God's power. He recreates this scene by means of words. In the storm that is real the poet senses a higher power that has revealed itself. This revelation provokes both fear and fascination. The storm begins either in the Mediterranean Sea or "the waters" (v. 3), that is, the ocean above the firmament-protected earth. In verses 5-9a this powerful storm now invades the earth. It leaps over Lebanon, goes under Sirion (the Phoenician name for Mount Hermon), passes to the wilderness, and penetrates the forest. The cracking and splintering of cedars, the flames of fire, the convulsing earth, and the tireless voice come together to provide an image of immense power.

This divine power, however, demands recognition. In verse 9b all acknowledge the Lord's "glory," that quality by which God manifests his presence on earth. Here it is a royal quality. In verse 10 the Lord sits enthroned in his temple that is above the firmament ("the flood"). In the Jerusalem temple, therefore, Israel experiences in a very tangible way the transcendent One whose dwelling is elsewhere. At the same time this presence is linked to something concrete. Peace (v. 11) is not merely the cessation of hostilities but the condition of wholeness whereby living becomes celebration.

The inherent temptation of the fertility religion of the Canaanites for the Israelites now takes the not too subtle form of technology. Given this climate, we must dare to let this psalm impact our technological world. It must put us in contact with the power of our God. Despite our enormous scientific breakthroughs, we must not outgrow our capacity to experience the mystery of God. Here is an awesome God who is not subject to the caprices of our successes. Here is a God who speaks to us through nature and other humans. Prayer must become that enterprise whereby we discover the manifold presence of this God once again. With such rediscoveries we enter upon a world where all needs are met and hence living is truly celebration. Such is the task of prayer.

## Psalm 100
## Processional Hymn

[1]A psalm of thanksgiving.
Shout joyfully to the LORD, all you lands;
  [2]serve the LORD with gladness;
  come before him with joyful song.

³Know that the LORD is God,
    he made us, we belong to him,
    we are his people, the flock he shepherds.
⁴Enter his gates with thanksgiving,
    his courts with praise.
Give thanks to him, bless his name;
    ⁵good indeed is the LORD,
His mercy endures forever,
    his faithfulness lasts through every generation.

This simple but powerful hymn actually consists of two minihymns: (1) verses 1-3 and (2) verses 4-5. Verses 1-2 and verse 4 constitute the call to praise while verse 3 and verse 5 provide the motivation. The first minihymn occurs as the worshipers are processing to the temple. The second minihymn takes place as they are entering through the courtyard gates. Most likely this psalm accompanied a thanksgiving service (see Lev 7:12-15). The note of exuberant joy characterizes the whole composition.

In verse 3 Israel worships the Lord as the shepherd or leader who acts on behalf of his people. Israel finds this identity in the exodus, that involvement that made Israel God's people and God's flock. This recollection of God's saving action leads to Israel's statement of loyalty. It is only the Lord who is truly God (v. 3) while all other claimants lack credentials. In such a climate it is only fitting that all the lands (v. 1) should honor the Lord. Finally in verse 5 Israel sings of the Lord's fidelity. "Good" implies enduring friendship while covenant love ("mercy") and faithfulness express the Lord's commitment to abide by his pledged word to Israel.

At prayer we must raise the troubling question of alternative loyalties and false perceptions of reality. Is the Lord alone truly our God or do we also worship the false gods of power and pleasure? Our participation in worship provides the occasion for our pledge of allegiance: "I believe in one God . . ." A genuine perception of reality implies that we take this pledge that God rules the world, not merely as individuals but also as a community. In either case we are not our own since we belong to the Lord (see 1 Cor 6:19). We are called upon to make our acceptance of the Lord alive and meaningful for others. Our faith must be a contagious force that impacts "all you lands" (v. 1).

**Psalm 65**
**Thanksgiving for God's Blessings**

[1]For the leader. A psalm of David. A song.

I

[2]To you we owe our hymn of praise,
    O God on Zion;
To you our vows must be fulfilled,
    [3]you who hear our prayers.
To you all flesh must come
    [4]with its burden of wicked deeds.
We are overcome by our sins;
    only you can pardon them.
[5]Blessed the one whom you will choose and bring
    to dwell in your courts.
May we be filled with the good things of your house,
    your holy temple!

II

[6]You answer us with awesome deeds of justice,
    O God our savior,
The hope of all the ends of the earth
    and of those far off across the sea.
[7]You are robed in power,
    you set up the mountains by your might.
[8]You still the roaring of the seas,
    the roaring of their waves,
    the tumult of the peoples.
[9]Distant peoples stand in awe of your marvels;
    the places of morning and evening you make resound with joy.
[10]You visit the earth and water it,
    make it abundantly fertile.
God's stream is filled with water;
    you supply their grain.
Thus do you prepare it:
    [11]you drench its plowed furrows,
    and level its ridges.
With showers you keep it soft,
    blessing its young sprouts.

¹²You adorn the year with your bounty;
    your paths drip with fruitful rain.
¹³The meadows of the wilderness also drip;
    the hills are robed with joy.
¹⁴The pastures are clothed with flocks,
    the valleys blanketed with grain;
    they cheer and sing for joy.

Zion, the oldest part of Jerusalem, came to be known as the City of David. That name was then applied to the entire enlarged city. However, is the Lord who has his temple on Zion and who controls the world and its history still interested in the day-to-day affairs of ordinary humans? This question may be put another way. Besides the glory of the temple and the control of the universe, is there another motive, indeed a more mundane motive, for praising God? The arrangement of this psalm offers an answer: (1) the attraction of Zion (vv. 2-5); (2) the Lord of the universe and history (vv. 6-9); (3) the Lord as farmer (vv. 10-14).

Mount Zion attracts both praise and supplication. It beckons to all who wish to experience intimacy with God, especially because of human sinfulness (vv. 2-4). In the heart of Zion, namely, the temple, Israel recalls the mystery of election—this people has been chosen to enter God's house (v. 5).

From Zion the psalmist now glances at the immense horizons of nature and history. The God of the sanctuary is the God of a people— indeed, an oppressed people (v. 6). In verses 7-8 the psalmist recalls the Lord's ongoing creative activity. Setting up the mountains and stilling the roaring of the seas recall the story of creation whereby the Lord overcame chaos and established order. Even though the nations perpetually gather their armies against Israel, the Lord continues to keep them in check (v. 8).

At this point the psalmist gives the impression that God has left the public arena to devote himself to farming (vv. 10-11). The God who checks kingdoms, restrains oceans, and receives praise in the temple also farms the land. Thus the God of the temple and the God of nature and history is also the concerned head of the household who provides for the needs of family members (vv. 12-13). The flocks on the hills and the grain in the valleys (v. 14) are eloquent witness to the Lord's attention to day-to-day needs. This psalm calls for a heightened sense of wonder and a more exuberant display of recognition of the God-given reliability of life. Given such rich agricultural productivity, the only adequate response is praise.

At prayer we are often tempted to focus on the great moments in our lives. Psalm 65, however, teaches us to look to the small moments as well, to the times of normalcy and humdrum affairs. We somehow feel reluctant to consider our jobs, whether they be in the office or factory, at home, on the farm, or wherever. Frequently we do not regard our positions as faith opportunities, occasions to acknowledge a God who gives us health and talent.

In the other direction we do not consider sufficiently those who meet our daily needs and hence those who work hand in hand with our God to provide for us. The tragedy is that we take human love for granted. Being in the temple or in control of the world seems more important than being down on the farm. At prayer we are to count our blessings: our jobs, our abilities, but most of all our loved and loving ones. Prayer is the chance to reassess the humdrum and rediscover divine presence through human love. Prayer makes us aware of the equilibrium that only love provides.

## Psalm 113
## Praise of God's Care for the Poor

¹Hallelujah!

I

Praise, you servants of the LORD,
    praise the name of the LORD.
²Blessed be the name of the LORD
    both now and forever.
³From the rising of the sun to its setting
    let the name of the LORD be praised.

II

⁴High above all nations is the LORD;
    above the heavens his glory.
⁵Who is like the LORD our God,
    enthroned on high,
        ⁶looking down on heaven and earth?

⁷He raises the needy from the dust,
    lifts the poor from the ash heap,
⁸Seats them with princes,
    the princes of the people,
⁹Gives the childless wife a home,
    the joyful mother of children.
Hallelujah!

Creation is not the only motive for praising the God of Israel. The Lord's actions on behalf of his people are equally significant. This implies that the Lord's heavenly court does not resemble the former Berlin Wall, eliminating his concern as to how the other half lives. Indeed covenant loyalty demands that this God be closely linked to the people and be committed to action on their behalf.

This psalm opens by inviting the Lord's servants to praise their God. Although "servants" can refer to temple personnel, it also extends to all Israel (see Ps 69:36-37). Verses 1-3, by accentuating the name of the Lord, focus on the person of Israel's God. According to Exodus 3:13-17 and 6:2-8 the revelation of the divine name takes place in the setting of Egyptian bondage. To mention "the Lord" is to conjure up the picture of a God who liberates slaves and offers them a future in a promised land. The expression "From the rising of the sun to its setting" (v. 3) refers to the Diaspora, that is, those Jews scattered throughout the ancient Near East after the exile (after 539 BC). However, where the divine name is revered, there the divine person is involved.

We never stand so tall as when we stoop to help a little child. The psalmist develops this theology in the body of the poem (vv. 4-9a) by underlining the chasm separating the Lord and his servants. However, it is a chasm that can be overcome. To be sure, the Lord is "[h]igh above all nations" (v. 4) and incomparable as he occupies his lofty throne (v. 5). Nevertheless he bends down to inspect the situation in heaven and on earth (v. 6). But this inspection is not another committee report—it is directed to action.

Who are the beautiful people? According to this psalm there are at least two categories: (1) the needy and the poor and (2) the childless wife. In both cases reversal is the order of the day. The One on high (v. 4) raises on high the needy and the poor. They occupy seats along with the princes of God's people. The movement from dust and ash heap is possible because the God of the covenant is loyal and, therefore, committed. With regard to the barren wife one must note that in the sociology of Israel a woman found fulfillment by becoming a wife and a mother, preferably of sons. She thus contributed to the covenant community by bearing children. The accounts of Israel's matriarchs are enough to point up the plight of the unfulfilled wife (see Gen 16:1-16; 30:1-24). But thanks to the Lord's intervention, the barren are no longer sullen. They break out into expressions of spontaneous joy because the Lord has removed their stigma by giving them children (v. 9; see 1 Sam 2:5). It is only fitting that the psalm should conclude as it began: "Hallelujah!" ("Praise Yahweh!").

This psalm obviously does not offer an exhaustive list of the marginalized. However, it does suggest to our imagination that wherever the marginalized find relief, the name of the Lord is present and demands recognition. In praying this psalm and ones like it, we are to acknowledge those individuals who reach out from their security or insecurity to lend a helping hand. Divine presence takes many forms. To help fellow humans in any way is to make God's name contagious and hence worthy of praise. At prayer we are urged to break free from the grip of our ego to focus on those who demonstrate freedom by giving themselves to others. To praise them is to demolish the barrier we erect even in prayer. To pray to this God is to be involved with this God's concern—everyone.

## Psalm 145
### The Greatness and Goodness of God

[1]Praise. Of David.
I will extol you, my God and king;
    I will bless your name forever and ever.
[2]Every day I will bless you;
    I will praise your name forever and ever.
[3]Great is the LORD and worthy of much praise,
    whose grandeur is beyond understanding.
[4]One generation praises your deeds to the next
    and proclaims your mighty works.
[5]They speak of the splendor of your majestic glory,
    tell of your wonderful deeds.

⁶They speak of the power of your awesome acts
    and recount your great deeds.
⁷They celebrate your abounding goodness
    and joyfully sing of your justice.
⁸The LORD is gracious and merciful,
    slow to anger and abounding in mercy.
⁹The LORD is good to all,
    compassionate toward all your works.
¹⁰All your works give you thanks, LORD
    and your faithful bless you.
¹¹They speak of the glory of your reign
    and tell of your mighty works,
¹²Making known to the sons of men your mighty acts,
    the majestic glory of your rule.
¹³Your reign is a reign for all ages,
    your dominion for all generations.
The LORD is trustworthy in all his words,
    and loving in all his works.
¹⁴The LORD supports all who are falling
    and raises up all who are bowed down.
¹⁵The eyes of all look hopefully to you;
    you give them their food in due season.
¹⁶You open wide your hand
    and satisfy the desire of every living thing.
¹⁷The LORD is just in all his ways,
    merciful in all his works.
¹⁸The LORD is near to all who call upon him,
    to all who call upon him in truth.
¹⁹He fulfills the desire of those who fear him;
    he hears their cry and saves them.
²⁰The LORD watches over all who love him,
    but all the wicked he destroys.
²¹My mouth will speak the praises of the LORD;
    all flesh will bless his holy name forever and ever.

This psalm is an acrostic, that is, a composition in which the initial letters of each verse form a pattern—here the letters of the Hebrew alphabet. It is also a representative expression of Israel's joy in the

Creator. The structure of the psalm seems to follow these lines: (1) praise of God's greatness (vv. 1-10); (2) God's everlasting kingship (vv. 11-13); (3) God's universal generosity (vv. 14-21).

In the first section, verses 8-9 are particularly significant. They are a statement of the Lord's main attributes: gracious, merciful, slow to anger, abounding in mercy, good to all, compassionate. This lineup is reminiscent of Exodus 34:6-7, where the covenant God is described as "The LORD, the LORD, a God gracious and merciful, slow to anger and abounding in love and fidelity, continuing his love for a thousand generations." The words "merciful" (v. 8) and "compassionate" (v. 9) derive from the Hebrew word for "womb." Hence the Lord experiences maternal tenderness for the child of her womb.

In the second section the psalmist focuses on God's kingship: rule, reign, dominion. As king (v. 1), the Lord has assumed the obligation of providing for his subjects. This is a kingship that will last forever.

In the third section the poet devotes his attention in large measure to the special concerns of God: those falling and bowed down (v. 14). What is significant is the author's concentration on God's universal care—the word "all" appears in verses 14, 15, 18, 20 and "every" in verse 16. A somewhat jarring note surfaces in verse 20. There the Lord who watches over all who love him also destroys all the wicked. In the orderliness depicted in this psalm, action against the wicked is justified. This is a God who keeps everything in proper alignment.

The divine world of this psalm clearly clashes with our overly autonomous human world. In this psalm God reigns supreme but it is an exercise of power that promotes the good of others. In reciting God's mighty works and his wonderful deeds, the psalmist invites the community to praise these accomplishments that benefit the common good. At the same time the poet implicitly urges them to imitate this example of sovereignty in their domain.

At prayer we may choose to focus on God's compassion and universalism. This is a God who feels intensely for the child of her womb. By the same token this is a God who experiences concern for all her children. This may give us pause as we reflect on our own situation. While we must exercise justice, we must also temper it with compassion. Because we are human, we tend to pick and choose. This psalm, however, suggests that we imitate our God who gives to all and provides for all.

## *New Testament*

Claus Westermann has remarked that all the psalms of descriptive praise are governed by a certain tension. On the one hand, God is enthroned in majesty. On the other hand, God is moved to compassion. He further suggests that the two parts of the prologue of the Gospel of John (1:1-13; 1:14-18) exemplify this tension. The following remarks are intended as aids in praying this segment of the New Testament.

### John 1:1-18

¹In the beginning was the Word,
    and the Word was with God,
    and the Word was God.
²He was in the beginning with God.
³All things came to be through him,
    and without him nothing came to be.
What came to be ⁴through him was life,
    and this life was the light of the human race;
⁵the light shines in the darkness,
    and the darkness has not overcome it.
⁶A man named John was sent from God. ⁷He came for testimony, to testify to the light, so that all might believe through him. ⁸He was not the light, but came to testify to the light. ⁹The true light, which enlightens everyone, was coming into the world.
¹⁰He was in the world,
    and the world came to be through him,
    but the world did not know him.
¹¹He came to what was his own,
    but his own people did not accept him.
¹²But to those who did accept him he gave power to become children of God, to those who believe in his name, ¹³who were born not by natural generation nor by human choice nor by a man's decision but of God.
¹⁴And the Word became flesh
    and made his dwelling among us,
    and we saw his glory,
    the glory as of the Father's only Son,
    full of grace and truth.

<sup>15</sup>John testified to him and cried out, saying, "This was he of whom I said, 'The one who is coming after me ranks ahead of me because he existed before me.'" <sup>16</sup>From his fullness we have all received, grace in place of grace, <sup>17</sup>because while the law was given through Moses, grace and truth came through Jesus Christ. <sup>18</sup>No one has ever seen God. The only Son, God, who is at the Father's side, has revealed him.

The prologue of John is a hymn that is probably an independent composition attached to the gospel. Moreover, an editor or editors have added to the hymn by inserting materials to explain the hymn more fully (vv. 12b-13, 17-18) and to differentiate the roles of Jesus and John the Baptist (vv. 6-9, 15). The title "Word" has wisdom overtones, that is, it smacks of books such as Proverbs and Wisdom. Thus the Word is like Lady Wisdom who is with God before creation (Prov 8:22-23), who reflects God's glory and everlasting light (Wis 7:25-26), and who provokes decisions (Prov 8:17).

The hymn begins with the period before creation and the Word's relationship to God. Through creation ("In the beginning"; see Gen 1:1), which is also a revelation, the Word has a claim on everyone. The effect of God's creative Word is the gift of eternal life. Although humans have failed through sin, the light continues to shine in darkness. Verses 11-12a describe the ministry of the Word and reach a crescendo in verse 14, where the Word is bound up with human history and human destiny. Westermann notes further that this descriptive praise leads into emphasis on God's new provision (". . . and we saw his glory . . . From his fullness we have all received . . .").

At prayer we are compelled to recognize God's movement as ever going forward. In the period before creation there is movement between God and the Word. In creation there is movement between the Word and the world of nature and humans. At the moment of God becoming human there is the ultimate movement between the Word and fragile humanity. At prayer we are caught up in this series of movements. We see ourselves as the beneficiaries of God's ongoing goodness; we see other humans as the empowered ambassadors of the Word. At prayer we must be overawed by such a generous God who makes his world impact ours. In the presence of the Word we are left speechless. Balance and harmony mean that the movement continues, becoming enfleshed in both our prayer and lifestyle.

## *Summary of the theology of the psalms of descriptive praise*

1. These psalms speak of divine intervention and human interaction. They are an appeal to praise our God for ongoing creation.
2. They assume that we humans can recognize our God both in nature and history. They also assume that we are able to put aside our focus on self to concentrate on the Faithful One.
3. They seek to celebrate the goodness of life because of the Giver of life.
4. They exhort us to announce the death of self and proclaim the good news of focus on God and the world of fellow humans.
5. They appeal to our ability to recognize the reality of ongoing creation in other people. The God of Israel seldom chooses to operate alone. To praise the cocreators is to praise the Creator.

# CHAPTER 3

# In God We Trust
## The Psalms of Trust or Confidence

*Human progress versus divine reliance*

Our technological age has witnessed unimagined wonders. The advances in medicine, aerospace engineering, and information systems have established new parameters for human confidence. Generally speaking, we have grown to rely on things: pills, smartphones, tablets, to name only a few. Our world is one of instant replay. We press buttons or click icons and instantaneously retrieve past events. Whether we wish to admit it or not, we are in danger of total reliance on things. Humans do not function, so we surmise, as adroitly or as perfectly as the products of our technological genius. Our temptation is to mint a new American penny and substitute "In things only do we trust."

To be sure, these are temptations and dangers but they are not insuperable. We need not oppose human progress and divine (or human) reliance; they can be complementary. In both we seek stability, harmony, and a regular flow in the rhythm of our lives. However, if we are to remain genuinely human, we must be willing to run the risk of grounding ourselves in Another who in turn runs the risk of calling us and other people to the enterprise of trust. We must be courageous enough to accept scientific advances and label them good, very good, but also bold enough to acknowledge that we are caught up in the mystery of our God. The great heroes and heroines seem to be those who can opt for "both-and" rather than "either-or" in this great venture of modern living.

At prayer we experience the mystery of our God. We begin to realize that the good things of human technology must be a help in approaching our God, not a hindrance. We further perceive that things can never be a substitute for persons, whether our God or other humans. Our God is not a neatly packaged item of our productive ingenuity. Our God is one who freely enters into our lives and the lives of others. This is a God who offers us a greater challenge than that of our technological break-throughs. This is a God who dares us to trust him, to be rooted in him, and thereby to find stability and harmony in our lives. This is also a God who freely chooses to depend on humans in creating this climate of trust. The God of the Bible is one who provokes confidence.

## Psalms of trust or confidence

These psalms reflect a state of spiritual balance and of satisfaction without smugness. In such psalms there is an unwavering, unruffled steadiness of complete confidence. Because of this attitude, certain motifs regularly emerge: for example, security like that of the infant nestling on its mother's lap (Ps 131:2), intimacy with God (Ps 16:9-11), as well as absolute and exclusive attachment to this God (Ps 125:1-2). This is indeed a world of orientation.

These psalms probably developed from the psalms of lament. They are the motives of confidence in the laments that have now become full-fledged psalms of their own. It is the predominance of the expressions of trust and confidence that distinguishes them from the laments. With regard to structure there is no consistent arrangement. Rather, the psalmist reiterates the different images and symbols of the all-encompassing presence of the God of Israel.

### Psalm 23
### The Lord, Shepherd and Host

¹A psalm of David.
I
The LORD is my shepherd;
    there is nothing I lack.

²In green pastures he makes me lie down;
 to still waters he leads me;
  ³he restores my soul.
He guides me along right paths
 for the sake of his name.
⁴Even though I walk through the valley of the shadow of death,
 I will fear no evil, for you are with me;
  your rod and your staff comfort me.
 II
⁵You set a table before me
 in front of my enemies;
You anoint my head with oil;
 my cup overflows.
⁶Indeed, goodness and mercy will pursue me
 all the days of my life;
I will dwell in the house of the LORD
 for endless days.

For many people this is the best-known and most utilized psalm in the entire book of Psalms. Its universal appeal stems from its combination of simplicity and richness. It contains two basic images: (1) shepherd (vv. 1-4) and (2) host (vv. 5-6). However, both images are set against the background of the desert. The protector of the sheep is also the protector of the traveler, who provides hospitality in his tent as well as security against all the enemies of the desert. To know such a shepherd-host is to know security.

The term "shepherd" also has political overtones that heighten the sense of protection and equilibrium. In the ancient Near East kings were commonly called shepherds. This implied that they found their proper identity by meeting the needs of their people. "Shepherd" implies, therefore, a total concern for and dedication to others (see Isa 40:11; Jer 23:1-4; Ezek 34:1-31). Here the psalmist links the connotation of shepherd with the dynamism of the Lord's name. According to verse 3 the Lord guides for the honor of his name. Fidelity to his name and hence fidelity to his covenant commitment compels the Lord to take more than a passing interest in his sheep.

By selecting a few concrete verbs, the psalmist evokes the whole character of pastoral concern ("lie down," "leads," "guides"). Green pastures and still waters (v. 2) reveal the Lord as provider, leader, and sustainer. The rod (v. 4) is a defensive weapon against wild animals. The staff (v. 4) is a support for the shepherd as he patiently urges on the grazing sheep. On occasion the shepherd will employ both rod and staff against the lagging or straying sheep. Hence both rod and staff are symbols of wholehearted concern and dedication. We are not surprised, therefore, that the sheep are without fear (v. 4).

The host image contrasts with but also complements the shepherd image. Here the Lord performs the amenities of a host: setting a table and anointing the head (v. 5). Significantly these gestures occur "in front of my enemies" (v. 5). It is tempting to see these enemies as the former opponents of the psalmist. In such a scenario the enemies witness the reversal that has taken place. Instead of being harassed, the guest of the Lord enjoys all the comforts of desert hospitality. For the enemies there is not the thrill of victory but the agony of defeat.

"[G]oodness and mercy" (v. 6) is an expression that captures the implications of covenant commitment. "Mercy" (perhaps better translated as "steadfast love/loyalty") connotes the Lord's abiding fidelity because of his covenant relationship. It is the assurance that God's willingness to provide will be demonstrated in a concrete way. "Goodness" conjures up dimensions of friendship and good relations that flow from the covenant bond. Although this protestation of divine care occurs in the Lord's house (v. 6), the psalmist need not necessarily belong to the temple personnel. This verse may simply be interpreted as the ongoing assurance of the Lord's presence.

We are not surprised that Psalm 23 finds a conspicuous place in funeral celebrations. On such occasions we pray for the comfort of the deceased and for his or her abiding presence with our God. In so doing, we express all those dimensions of harmony and unruffledness that are so typical of the psalms of trust or confidence. It is a peace that is remote from our hectic business world.

Covenant, however, is a two-edged sword. It challenges us in this instance not only to experience our own personal harmony and rootedness in God but also to reach out and be the catalysts of trust and hope for others. To be in covenant with this God means to sustain this God's people. Pursuing the analogy of the funeral, we must employ Psalm 23 not only for the deceased but also for the bereaved. Setting a table (v. 5) means more than providing a meal after the services. Lying down in green pastures (v. 2) implies more than attending the wake. In our communing with our God we are urged to share our harmony and peace with others. Our task is not to explain the mystery of death and theologize about God's justice. In genuine prayer that breaks free of the kneeler or prie-dieu and invades the world, our duty is to be a staff for others to lean on and a rod to move on gently with the sorrowing. Our bold reliance on our covenant God and our sense of ease in his presence imply that we make our prayer actively contagious for the less than courageous and those ill at ease.

## Psalm 11
### Confidence in the Presence of God

¹For the leader. Of David.

I

In the LORD I take refuge;
> how can you say to me,
> "Flee like a bird to the mountains!
²See how the wicked string their bows,
> fit their arrows to the string
> to shoot from the shadows at the upright of heart.
³If foundations are destroyed,
> what can the just one do?"

II

⁴The LORD is in his holy temple;
> the LORD's throne is in heaven.
God's eyes keep careful watch;
> they test the children of Adam.
⁵The LORD tests the righteous and the wicked,
> hates those who love violence,
⁶And rains upon the wicked
> fiery coals and brimstone,
> a scorching wind their allotted cup.
⁷The LORD is just and loves just deeds;
> the upright will see his face.

Our human experience attests that injustice flourishes and that violence done to the poor is frequently not redressed. Corruption even invades our courts and seduces our judicial personnel. Not even our supreme courts are necessarily the ultimate bastions for dispensing justice to all. Perhaps without articulating it, we raise this question deep within our anguished spirit: Is there any final source that will mete out justice to the wronged and punishment to the guilty?

The setting for this psalm seems to be the temple. A persecuted innocent man flees to God's house and invokes the right of asylum. The temple employees inform him that the temple does not provide absolutely certain asylum. They advise him, therefore, to flee to the mountains like a bird (v. 1). He reacts to such advice by professing his unshakeable confidence in the judgment of the Lord (vv. 4-7). When the foundations of public order are overthrown (v. 3), the ultimate hope of justice resides with the Lord.

The author sets up a tension between the Lord and the persecuted innocent person. According to verse 7 the Lord is just and in verse 5 the Lord tests the righteous, hence the psalmist. There is another tension between light and darkness. In verse 2 the wicked shoot their arrows at the upright from the shadows. However, according to verse 4 God's eyes pierce the darkness, exposing everyone and everything. Finally there is a tension with regard to punishment. In verse 2 the wicked string their bows and shoot their arrows. But in verse 6 the Lord reaches into his own arsenal to mete out justice: fiery coals, brimstone, and a scorching wind.

The divine throne, the mountains, and the temple develop the psalmist's views of presence and thus security. God's throne is a law tribunal (v. 4). Heaven (v. 4) shows that this throne is the supreme court where the Lord examines all humans without distinction (vv. 4-5). In turn, what makes the temple secure is the presence of the Lord. The mountains (v. 1) enter this pattern of refuge only in order to be rejected. It is only the Lord who is the final source of genuine security. In the end the just person realizes that injustice and violence will not be the last word. There is always the Lord, the ultimate court of appeal. Though human courts may fail, this final court of appeal in heaven is totally reliable and dependable.

At prayer we enjoy our own legal system where the Lawyer does not ask, "Can you pay?" but "In what way may I serve you?" This realization affords security and confidence. In the presence of this God there is no question of wiretapping or phone bugging. Ours is a God who knows the situation even before we attempt to explain it to ourselves.

Ultimately our sense of redress and administration of justice does not reside in a system but in a Person. At prayer we are not involved in legal maneuvers but with a Person who soothes the pain of rejection and the ignominy of exclusion. We do not lick our wounds. Rather, there is Another who binds them up, pouring in oil and wine (see Luke 10:34).

Like Psalm 23, this psalm must help us not merely to find security with Another but to be security for others. Like the psalmist, we are exhorted to reject flight and take a stand precisely when everything seems to be falling apart. We must recall that the God who pampers us in his sanctuary is also the God who empowers us in the marketplace. We simply cannot look on complacently when the foundations of justice are overthrown and people, especially the poor, are the victims. At prayer we are challenged to denounce all those "systems" that choose to remain anonymous so that those suffering may bring no charges against them. To be in covenant means to sustain the weakest in covenant. Genuine justice is in session with the Lord presiding only when the reciters of Psalm 11 translate their personal experience of exoneration into meaningful action for all those denied their rights. Because of covenant, our prayer necessarily has community overtones.

## Psalm 27
## Trust in God

[1]Of David.

A

I

The LORD is my light and my salvation;
　　whom should I fear?
The LORD is my life's refuge;
　　of whom should I be afraid?
[2]When evildoers come at me
　　to devour my flesh,
These my enemies and foes
　　themselves stumble and fall.
[3]Though an army encamp against me,
　　my heart does not fear;
Though war be waged against me,
　　even then do I trust.

II

⁴One thing I ask of the LORD;
    this I seek:
To dwell in the LORD's house
    all the days of my life,
To gaze on the LORD's beauty,
    to visit his temple.
⁵For God will hide me in his shelter
    in time of trouble,
He will conceal me in the cover of his tent;
    and set me high upon a rock.
⁶Even now my head is held high
    above my enemies on every side!
I will offer in his tent
    sacrifices with shouts of joy;
    I will sing and chant praise to the LORD.

B

I

⁷Hear my voice, LORD, when I call;
    have mercy on me and answer me.
⁸"Come," says my heart, "seek his face";
    your face, LORD, do I seek!
⁹Do not hide your face from me;
    do not repel your servant in anger.
You are my salvation; do not cast me off;
    do not forsake me, God my savior!
¹⁰Even if my father and mother forsake me,
    the LORD will take me in.

II

¹¹LORD, show me your way;
    lead me on a level path
    because of my enemies.
¹²Do not abandon me to the desire of my foes;
    malicious and lying witnesses have risen against me.
¹³I believe I shall see the LORD's goodness
    in the land of the living.
¹⁴Wait for the LORD, take courage;
    be stouthearted, wait for the LORD!

Although this psalm may seem to be two psalms (vv. 1-6 = psalm of trust or confidence; vv. 7-14 = psalm of lament), the overriding motif (even in the lament) is that of unwavering trust. Hence, as a whole, it illustrates the stage of orientation.

Verse 1 is actually the premise of the entire piece: the Lord is light, salvation, and refuge. Hence fear is out of the question. Verses 2-3 illustrate the threats confronting the psalmist but only in a general way: evildoers, enemies, foes, encamped army. The only yearning the author has is for the assurance of God's presence in the temple. For the people of Israel the temple is like paradise revisited. There they eat, drink, and sing (v. 6). God's face or presence in the temple (vv. 8-9) is the very bedrock of confidence. The author describes this sense of reliability by use of such images as shelter, tent, and rock (v. 5).

Such trust does not eliminate life's problems and troubles. The psalmist expresses this situation by the use of imperatives: hear, have mercy, answer (v. 7); not hide, not repel, not cast off, not forsake (v. 9); show, lead (v. 11); not abandon (v. 12). The need for such cries is balanced by trust in a savior (v. 9) who surpasses even parents for providing help (v. 10). The psalm concludes with an oracle of salvation (perhaps spoken by the priest in the temple) that underlines the need for waiting, taking courage, and being stouthearted (v. 14).

The general character of the problems besetting the psalmist is really a boon. For us, evildoers, enemies, and foes can easily become concrete figures at prayer. Loss of health, death of a loved one, breakup of a relationship, and so forth, are very real problems that we often experience. In the very midst of these concerns we are reminded that there is One who invites us to trust, to anchor our lives totally in him. While we wait for the Lord (v. 14), we can anticipate our God's willing response.

Looking to the problems of others, we must feel ourselves compelled to offer the ministry of divine presence. It is that presence, particularly in the temple, that serves as the basis of the psalmist's hope. In turn, we must make God present to others. The temple gives way to home, work, or social life, where many may not sense presence but absence. We are to make light and salvation available through compassion and comfort. It is such presence that makes the shouts of joy possible.

**Psalm 63**
**Ardent Longing for God**

¹A psalm of David, when he was in the wilderness of Judah.

I

²O God, you are my God—
  it is you I seek!
For you my body yearns;
  for you my soul thirsts,
In a land parched, lifeless,
  and without water.
³I look to you in the sanctuary
  to see your power and glory.
⁴For your love is better than life;
  my lips shall ever praise you!

II

⁵I will bless you as long as I live;
  I will lift up my hands, calling on your name.
⁶My soul shall be sated as with choice food,
  with joyous lips my mouth shall praise you!

⁷I think of you upon my bed,
  I remember you through the watches of the night.
⁸You indeed are my savior,
  and in the shadow of your wings I shout for joy.
⁹My soul clings fast to you;
  your right hand upholds me.

III

¹⁰But those who seek my life will come to ruin;
  they shall go down to the depths of the netherworld!
¹¹Those who would hand over my life to the sword shall
  become the prey of jackals!
¹²But the king shall rejoice in God;
  all who swear by the Lord shall exult,
  but the mouths of liars will be shut!

This exquisite psalm emphasizes the intimate bond between God and
the worshiper. Although at a distance from God (v. 2), the psalmist
passionately desires God's life-dispensing presence in the temple (vv.

3-6). Such an experience derives from the closeness of this mutual relationship (vv. 7-9). Finally the psalm concludes with the assurance that the wicked will be overcome and the righteous will continue to praise this loyal God (vv. 10-12).

Confidence and intimacy go hand in hand. The psalmist captures this intimacy by his use of images describing the painful absence of God: "In a land parched, lifeless, / and without water" (v. 2). Given this situation, it is understandable why the poet is yearning and thirsting for divine presence. Although there is no clear evidence for belief in an afterlife before the second century BC so that life itself is seen as the greatest good, here we learn that God's love is even better than life itself (v. 4). Furthermore, it is profound prayer that sustains this unique bond: the lifting up of hands (v. 5), the rich banquet of praise (v. 6), the shout for joy (v. 8). "[I]n the shadow of your wings" (v. 8) probably refers to the holy of holies in the temple where the cherubim with their outstretched wings flanked God's throne (see 1 Kgs 6:23-28; 8:6-7).

The psalmist's enemies will end up in the netherworld prematurely (v. 10). The sword will undo them and jackals will feast on them (v. 11). Finally the reactions of the righteous and the wicked will present a clear contrast. While the latter will be silenced, the former will sing their praise of this discriminating God (v. 12).

This prayer can serve as a litmus test of our loyalties. We must dare to ask: What do we value more than life itself? Perhaps almost immediately we will think of some very special loved ones. Our intimate relationship with them may be our greatest human asset. Or perhaps, instead of people, we will consider pleasure and power more important. Prayer provides a unique occasion for lining up our priorities. We are challenged to emulate the psalmist by declaring that God's love is greater than life itself. We are urged to believe in concrete ways that such love indeed conquers everything.

While Psalm 63 clearly underlines the intimacy between God and the worshiper, it does not exclude our concern for others. The more intimate we are with this God, the closer we become to this God's extended family. Even the most personal moments of our prayer life must embrace this wider family. In one way or another we must seek to make our sense of trust in this God a reality for them. After all, Psalm 63 is no longer a purely private prayer. It is the prayer of both the synagogue and the church.

**Psalm 16**
**God the Supreme Good**

¹A *miktam* of David.

I

Keep me safe, O God;
    in you I take refuge.
²I say to the LORD,
    you are my Lord,
    you are my only good.
³As for the holy ones who are in the land,
    they are noble,
    in whom is all my delight.
⁴They multiply their sorrows
    who court other gods.
Blood libations to them I will not pour out,
    nor will I take their names upon my lips.
⁵LORD, my allotted portion and my cup,
    you have made my destiny secure.
⁶Pleasant places were measured out for me;
    fair to me indeed is my inheritance.

II

⁷I bless the LORD who counsels me;
    even at night my heart exhorts me.
⁸I keep the LORD always before me;
    with him at my right hand, I shall never be shaken.
⁹Therefore my heart is glad, my soul rejoices;
    my body also dwells secure,
¹⁰For you will not abandon my soul to Sheol,
    nor let your devout one see the pit.
¹¹You will show me the path to life,
    abounding joy in your presence,
    the delights at your right hand forever.

This psalm (a "miktam" is probably a literary or musical term) may reflect the situation of a worshiper who suffers from a severe illness (vv. 7-10) but who in the end experiences healing (v. 11). In verses 1-6 there is a confession of faith in the Lord alone. In verses 7-11 there is an expression of confidence owing to recovery. Verse 1 ("Keep me safe") looks to verses 7-11. Verse 2 ("you are my Lord") points to verses 3-6.

Besides the danger of death the psalmist is aware of the danger of false gods. Confronted with this second danger, he confesses that the Lord is his only good (v. 2). He then affirms his loyalty to God's people by speaking of the holy ones, probably fellow Israelites who embody the notion of fidelity (v. 3). In verse 4 the author observes that worshipers of false gods only create more problems for themselves. Stalwart in his faith, the psalmist professes that he will not pronounce the names of these gods or make offerings to them. On the other hand the psalmist acknowledges that the Lord is his allotted portion and cup (v. 5). The inheritance (v. 6) alludes to the division of the Promised Land among the Israelites (see Josh 18:8, 10).

In celebrating his recovery, the psalmist testifies that God's presence makes him unshakeable, exuberant, and secure (vv. 8-9). In healing the psalmist, God preserved him from going down to the netherworld (v. 10: Sheol, the pit). The "path to life" (v. 11) seems to sum up the entire experience of the psalmist.

At prayer the mention of other gods in this psalm may be useful. We believers, though we usually do not subscribe to overt idolatry, do fashion other gods. They may be unbridled pleasure, rank individualism, or self-seeking power. A psalm such as Psalm 16 may help us to forge a balance between wholesome human drives, on the one hand, and the centrality of our God, on the other hand. This psalm may suggest to our prayerful imagination that imbalance sets in when these drives do not lead us to serve God and our community.

How do we use our prayer time when we deal with serious illness? While we must certainly use the ordinary means of preserving life, we are challenged by this psalm to see the Divine Healer involved in our distress. While our society fears the tiniest specter of death and makes frantic efforts to have it disappear, the stance of Psalm 16 offers a healthy alternative. Trust implies that this God calls us to see our health problems as a portion, cup, and destiny (v. 5). This is not the invocation of blind fate but the acknowledgment of divine presence. Confidence is an indispensable element in "the path to life" (v. 11).

## Psalm 121
## The Lord My Guardian

[1]A song of ascents.
I raise my eyes toward the mountains.
   From whence shall come my help?
[2]My help comes from the LORD,
   the maker of heaven and earth.
[3]He will not allow your foot to slip;
   or your guardian to sleep.
[4]Behold, the guardian of Israel
   never slumbers nor sleeps.
[5]The LORD is your guardian;
   the LORD is your shade
   at your right hand.
[6]By day the sun will not strike you,
   nor the moon by night.
[7]The LORD will guard you from all evil;
   he will guard your soul.
[8]The LORD will guard your coming and going
   both now and forever.

Psalms 120–134 are a special collection in the book of Psalms. They are called songs of ascent because they were used by pilgrims as they went up or "ascended" to Jerusalem. Although this collection consists of different types, it does contain certain common features. Joy-filled confidence in God, optimistic petitions for forgiveness, and thanksgivings for the Lord's bounty toward Israel are prominent in this collection. The psalmist takes a simple idea or image and develops it with an economy of words. These psalms do not intend to communicate an idea. They are, rather, lyrical, seeking to penetrate sweetly.

The prominent motif in Psalm 121 is the notion of guarding. The noun "guardian" and the verb "to guard" appear a total of six times. In developing this image, the psalmist introduces possible dangers. In verse 3 there is the danger of one's foot slipping or the Lord's sleeping. In verse 6 there is the danger of exposure to the powerful Palestinian sun as well as the danger of the superstitious impact of the moon. However, all these dangers are offset by the recurring image of guarding.

One must note that after using the first person in verses 1-2, the author switches to the second person in verse 3. Since no particular scene is described, scholars have made several suggestions, for example, a lonely sentinel making his rounds, an insomniac, or a person seeking help. Perhaps there is value in seeing the silence and solitude of the night as the scene.

In this scenario a person raises his eyes from the city and its walls to the natural defense of the surrounding mountains. His glance continues to the top of the mountains and reaches the heavens (v. 1). His thoughts are now on the Lord who made heaven and earth (v. 2). His glance has been the interrogator and now, having arrived at the heavens, receives a totally satisfying answer (vv. 3-8). The one at prayer has answered his own question, realizing that God guarantees the answer. The answer is basically a theology of concern. It is the assurance that the all-powerful creator of heaven and earth looks to the needs of one frail human being. Confidence consists in knowing that one is not a nameless face in a chaos of anonymity. There is indeed a God who does care.

One can pursue this impression of confidence and prolong it in a night scene where a mother cradles her child to sleep. The back-and-forth motion of the rocking lulls the child to sleep. Clearly there is no need for fear since the child senses the presence of its mother. Aware that its mother is watching and not dozing, the child can enjoy the rocking, close its eyes, and fall peacefully asleep.

At prayer we are asked to focus on the goodness of Another. While not dismissing our problems, we are urged to concentrate on One who gives and provides because it is this God's nature to give and provide. Our technological explosion notwithstanding, we are invited to delight in Another who accepts us with our limitations and our fears. The image of God as mother (see Num 11:11-12; Deut 32:18; Isa 66:7-11) comes immediately to mind. This is the God who nurses and sustains us without tabulating the costs just as mothers do not enter energy expenses into their computers when it is a question of their children. This is the God who protects and shelters us without calculating the risks just as mothers do not operate on the basis of reciprocal agreements. At prayer, therefore, we are to find delight and happiness. After such an experience, we can return to our world with renewed energy and zest because of the conviction that Another cares, especially through other covenant partners.

In the setting of covenant we are also to recall the many others in our lives who exercise the ministry of caring for us. We are to remember those people who demonstrate the maternal concern of our God when we are ill, when we are depressed, when we are down and out. But recollection must bear fruit in our revealing a God who relates to others. We are bidden to be guardians for those who make up the fabric of our lives. In this way our own experience of tranquillity and security becomes the catalyst for meeting the needs of others. Hence while we fall peacefully asleep in the arms of our God, we are also awake to the call for help coming from our God's other children.

### Psalm 131
### Humble Trust in God

[1]A song of ascents. Of David.
LORD, my heart is not proud;
    nor are my eyes haughty.
I do not busy myself with great matters,
    with things too sublime for me.
[2]Rather, I have stilled my soul,
Like a weaned child to its mother,
    weaned is my soul.
[3]Israel, hope in the LORD,
    now and forever.

This is certainly one of the most beautiful psalms of trust. The body of the psalm (vv. 1-2) consists of two statements, one negative and the other positive. In verse 1 there is the threefold negative statement: heart not proud, eyes not haughty, no pursuit of greatness and sublime matters. While the proud heart (see Prov 18:12) and haughty eyes (see Ps 18:28) suggest an arrogant autonomy that defies God, this verse implies the exact opposite. In verse 2 there is a positive statement. As a weaned child no longer calls frantically for its mother's milk but is quite content upon her lap, so is the psalmist. While both verses capture the attitude of submission and subordination, they also convey due recognition of the Lord and freedom from anxiety.

Verse 3 (probably an addition to the psalm) is a fitting application of the qualities and virtues of verses 1-2 to Israel. Israel is now presented as a weaned child who will no longer insist on going its own way but will surrender itself lovingly to the will of the Lord. It is this type of surrender that makes hope possible. It is autonomy and exclusive self-reliance that create hopelessness since they reject God's gifts. The use of the domestic images of verses 1-2 for the attitude of Israel implies that the addition of verse 3 is most appropriate.

Stress is a key word in our daily lives. This stress may derive in part from our drive toward total independence, wherein we equate freedom with autonomy. At prayer we may have to ask ourselves what role reliance on others plays in our lives. Psalm 131 recommends that childlike, not childish, surrender is still a great value.

Psalm 131 offers the image of the weaned child as a model for the people of Israel. At prayer we should perhaps recall the role models who profoundly influence our lives by their simplicity and joyful dedication. We may find ourselves challenged to imitate those virtues in our stressful environment. To emulate such qualities is also to appreciate the people who embody them.

## Psalm 62
## Trust in God Alone

¹For the leader; *'al Jeduthun.* A psalm of David.

I

²My soul rests in God alone,
    from whom comes my salvation.
³God alone is my rock and salvation,
    my fortress; I shall never fall.
⁴How long will you set yourself against a man?
    You shall all be destroyed,
Like a sagging wall
    or a tumbled down fence!
⁵Even highly placed people
    plot to overthrow him.
They delight in lies;
    they bless with their mouths,
    but inwardly they curse.

*Selah*

## II

<sup>6</sup>My soul, be at rest in God alone,
    from whom comes my hope.
<sup>7</sup>God alone is my rock and my salvation,
    my fortress; I shall not fall.
<sup>8</sup>My deliverance and honor are with God,
    my strong rock;
    my refuge is with God.
<sup>9</sup>Trust God at all times, my people!
    Pour out your hearts to God our refuge!

*Selah*

## III

<sup>10</sup>Mortals are a mere breath,
    the sons of man but an illusion;
On a balance they rise;
    together they weigh nothing.
<sup>11</sup>Do not trust in extortion;
    in plunder put no empty hope.
On wealth that increases,
    do not set your heart.
<sup>12</sup>One thing God has said;
    two things I have heard:
Strength belongs to God;
    <sup>13</sup>so too, my Lord, does mercy,
For you repay each man
    according to his deeds.

Will my real friends please stand up? Will my real values kindly make themselves known? Is there anyone who will prove to be totally reliable? These are the implicit questions that this psalm poses in its own meditative way. Like Psalm 121, this psalm does not speak *to* God but *about* God (with the exception of v. 13). It challenges the person at prayer to entertain questions about genuine values.

The psalm opens with an introduction about God (vv. 2-3). This then leads to a critique of values in verses 4-11. Trust in God (vv. 6-9) is bracketed by false friends/values (vv. 4-5) and human weakness (vv. 10-11). The psalm concludes with a statement of God's covenant fidelity (v. 13a) and a later addition (v. 13b).

For the psalmist God is the bastion of security who offers him (v. 2: "soul") victory. This security is reflected in the images of rock and fortress (v. 3) that lead to the conviction of never falling. What is significant is that "God alone" (vv. 2, 3) provides such reliability or certainty. The psalmist next reflects on his false friends by way of contrast. They oppress him (v. 4), intending only to bring about his destruction. Lies have become their way of life (v. 5). They say one thing (blessing) but mean another (curse). Again the refrain appears (vv. 6-7): "God alone" is the really dependable one. Hope resides solely in God.

In verse 8 the psalmist adds to the earlier images of security: deliverance, honor (literally, heaviness, hence reliability), and refuge. Turning now to the assembly of the faithful, the psalmist lets his experience have an impact on them. Only God serves as the ongoing source of trust (v. 9). On the other hand, all humans—both great and small—lack the stability of God; they are mere breath and an illusion (v. 10). The following, therefore, are not lasting values: extortion, plunder, increased wealth (v. 11). In the conclusion the psalmist insists that real strength belongs to God (v. 12). Moreover, the Lord is a practitioner of covenant values (v. 13a: "mercy"). According to verse 13b the Lord treats humans with justice. ("Selah" is usually thought to be a direction for the temple cantor or musicians. However, its precise meaning is not clear.)

The multiple images of trust or confidence in this psalm are compelling. "Rock" appears three times while "salvation," "fortress," and "refuge" all appear twice. The frequency of these images must impress us at prayer. This God is utterly dependable and reliable. He has more than adequate credentials.

At prayer we raise the question of values. Without putting down everyone, we realize that in not a few instances power is the name of the game. Wealth, prestige, position—to cite only a few—are judged to be manifestations of real power. However, according to Paul they are forms of that uncontrollable power unleashed upon the world since the time of the first sin (see Rom 5:12-21). Such forms pervert and manipulate, trying to suck humans down the vortex of their insatiable desires. The truth is that these desires are never totally satisfying. In one direction prayer forces us to assess our contribution to this power by our own sinfulness. In another direction prayer compels us to place our values in dependable persons, namely, our God and other humans to the extent that they are open to the good of fellow humans. Humans, after all, must be rock and refuge for other humans. In that way they share their own stability and dependability, reflecting the solidity of the Rock.

## Psalm 125
### Israel's Protector

[1]A song of ascents.
Those trusting in the LORD are like Mount Zion,
   unshakable, forever enduring.
[2]As mountains surround Jerusalem,
   the LORD surrounds his people
   both now and forever.
[3]The scepter of the wicked will not prevail
   in the land allotted to the just,
Lest the just themselves
   turn their hands to evil.
[4]Do good, LORD, to the good,
   to those who are upright of heart.
[5]But those who turn aside to crooked ways
   may the LORD send down with the evildoers.
Peace upon Israel!

This is a communal psalm of trust reflecting the situation of postexilic Judah (after 539 BC), namely, the occupation of the ancestral land by a foreign power. During the course of worship in the temple, God's faithful people prayerfully bring this concern (see Neh 9:36-37) to the Lord's attention. They assert that their security is as unassailable as the city of Jerusalem (Zion) itself (v. 1). This assertion is not grounded in their own self-confidence but in the Lord's promises (see Isa 58:13; 60:21). Just as mountains ring the Holy City, so the Lord will continue to protect his people.

Verse 3 introduces the contrast (also developed in vv. 4-5) of the wicked and the just. The wicked are faithless Jews or religiously indifferent Jews (see Isa 56:9–57:13). The just, however, are obedient members of God's people who are the heirs of the Promised Land that was divided by lot among the tribes (see Num 26:55; Josh 15:1). If the domination of the wicked were to go on, even the just would be victims of their sinfulness. Given this situation, the just ask that the Lord do good to the good, that is, those faithful to the covenant who are also described as upright of heart (v. 4). On the other hand, the just beseech the Lord to expel from the covenant community the unworthy Jews (those turning aside to crooked ways) together with the wicked, that is, evildoers, perhaps foreign patrons (v. 5). Despite this desperate situation, the faithful are confident of peace.

At prayer we cannot pretend that only goodness and justice exist in our world. We must admit that evil and injustice abound. In the midst of this mixed reality Psalm 125 reminds us that our God is not disinterested in our plight. We have precedents from our own history to prove that this God surrounds us as mountains surround Jerusalem. It is the pursuit of peace that must invade the quiet moments of prayer. Peace cannot be something merely to be desired but never attainable. Peace must be the preoccupation, indeed the obsession, of those who dare to pray to the Prince of Peace.

In terms of covenant we must also reflect on the need for modern Mount Zions. We believers have a mandate from our God to be refuge and strength for our sisters and brothers. By our involvement we are asked to inspire trust so that hope becomes genuine for the victims of evil and injustice. To trust in this God is to nurture trust for this God's people.

## Psalm 91
## Security Under God's Protection

I

¹You who dwell in the shelter of the Most High,
  who abide in the shade of the Almighty,
²Say to the LORD, "My refuge and fortress,
  my God in whom I trust."
³He will rescue you from the fowler's snare,
  from the destroying plague,
⁴He will shelter you with his pinions,
  and under his wings you may take refuge;
  his faithfulness is a protecting shield.
⁵You shall not fear the terror of the night
  nor the arrow that flies by day,

⁶Nor the pestilence that roams in darkness,
    nor the plague that ravages at noon.
⁷Though a thousand fall at your side,
    ten thousand at your right hand,
    near you it shall not come.
⁸You need simply watch;
    the punishment of the wicked you will see.
⁹Because you have the Lord for your refuge
    and have made the Most High your stronghold,
¹⁰No evil shall befall you,
    no affliction come near your tent.
¹¹For he commands his angels with regard to you,
    to guard you wherever you go.
¹²With their hands they shall support you,
    lest you strike your foot against a stone.
¹³You can tread upon the asp and the viper,
    trample the lion and the dragon.

II

¹⁴Because he clings to me I will deliver him;
    because he knows my name I will set him on high.
¹⁵He will call upon me and I will answer;
    I will be with him in distress;
    I will deliver him and give him honor.
¹⁶With length of days I will satisfy him,
    and fill him with my saving power.

How will the Lord intervene on my behalf? Specifically what kind of protection will this God grant me? In answer to these questions Psalm 91 uses a variety of images to concretize the manner and the kind of divine intervention and protection. It is possible to divide the psalm as follows: (1) an introduction (vv. 1-2) that welcomes the pilgrim to the sanctuary (v. 2 was possibly recited by the pilgrim); (2) a priestly sermonette of encouragement given in the sanctuary (vv. 3-13); (3) a final oracle given in God's name (vv. 14-16).

According to verses 3-4 intervention means release from the fowler's snare and immunization against a devastating plague. The Lord is described as a mighty bird who takes the pilgrim under his wings (see Exod 19:4; Deut 32:11). However, the Lord is also a powerful warrior.

His fidelity takes the form of the standard military hardware of a "protecting shield" (v. 4). In terms of danger verses 5-6 spell out four crises for four periods of time: (1) "terror of the night"; (2) arrow of the day; (3) pestilence at evening ("darkness"); (4) devastating plague at noon. God's presence means the absence of fear in the face of such formidable dangers. It is interesting to note that the psalmist balances these four crises of time with four animals in verse 13 (asp, viper, lion, and dragon).

Other images of divine protection as well as reward and punishment unfold in verses 7-12. The psalmist develops the plague of verse 3. According to verse 7, though innumerable people fall victim to the rampaging disease, the one trusting in the Lord has no reason to fear. Verses 8-10 contain a statement of the traditional belief in retribution: during this life the just will be vindicated for their loyalty while the wicked will certainly be punished. Finally in verses 11-12 the company of angels offers safety on the rocky roads of the Near East.

The psalm comes to a conclusion in verses 14-16, which may be an oracle spoken by a priest or some other official. In any event, these verses express the theology of the psalm: fidelity to God means deliverance from any and all forms of distress. "[S]aving power" (v. 16) is the concrete demonstration of divine concern and compassion in this world. In this psalm confidence presumes a black-and-white world where God responds to injustice with mathematical precision. This is indeed a world of order and equilibrium.

At prayer the imagery of this psalm must provoke a reaction. As the psalm develops, we perceive a variety of images, all calculated to conjure up security and protection: for example, the giant bird (v. 4), the mighty warrior (v. 4), the provider of heavenly company (v. 11). Perhaps we may be tempted to understand our God after the manner of Fort Knox, nuclear warfare, or the Pentagon. But putting aside these temptations, we are invited to test the theology of the biblical imagery and make it the springboard for our prayer, or at least certain dimensions of our prayer. We must learn anew each day that we must ground our lives in Another whose name and plan we know.

At prayer this psalm must remind us of Romans 8:39 that absolutely nothing "will be able to separate us from the love of God in Christ Jesus our Lord." Trust and love are complementary. To the extent that we love, to that degree we trust. This is not a blind trust but one grounded in the love of Jesus on the cross who continued to trust his Father (see Luke 23:46).

## New Testament

### Matthew 6:25-30

[25]"Therefore I tell you, do not worry about your life, what you will eat [or drink], or about your body, what you will wear. Is not life more than food and the body more than clothing? [26]Look at the birds in the sky; they do not sow or reap, they gather nothing into barns, yet your heavenly Father feeds them. Are not you more important than they? [27]Can any of you by worrying add a single moment to your life-span? [28]Why are you anxious about clothes? Learn from the way the wild flowers grow. They do not work or spin. [29]But I tell you that not even Solomon in all his splendor was clothed like one of them. [30]If God so clothes the grass of the field, which grows today and is thrown into the oven tomorrow, will he not much more provide for you, O you of little faith?"

In this section of his Sermon on the Mount Matthew calls upon his community to extricate itself from anxieties about daily needs (v. 25). Although this is not a psalm of trust or confidence, it reflects many of the characteristics of this psalm type. Neither biblical tradition advocates flight from concern about these real needs. Rather, the focus is on anxiety that implies total absorption in the goods of this world. Discipleship frees one to trust in the true Giver and Sustainer of life. In verses 26-29 Matthew presents examples confirming the Father's unrelenting care of the disciples. The Father feeds the birds and decks the wild flowers with a splendor greater than Solomon's royal robes. If, therefore, the Father devotes such attention to this passing world, will he not take greater care of his own family (v. 30)?

In the spirit of the psalms of trust or confidence Matthew hammers home the truth that we must run the risk of grounding ourselves in Another. By taking such a risk, we open ourselves to the realization that our God is genuinely interested in us as persons and that commitment to his pledged word means ongoing concern. Harmony and stability, therefore, do not come from a flight from the legitimate concerns of everyday life but from a concentration on the character of our God—*the* Giver (see also Matt 11:28-30).

In another passage Mathew exposes the covenant dimension of this trust or confidence, namely, concern for others. In the great scene of the last judgment (25:31-46) Matthew expounds the doctrine of harmony and contentment at that judging by focusing on the person of Jesus: "Amen, I say to you, whatever you did for one of these least brothers of mine, you did for me" (v. 40).

For Matthew Jesus is reflected in the hungry, the thirsty, the stranger, the naked, the sick, and the imprisoned. What is done for these and others like them is the criterion of judgment since it reveals one's basic behavior and relationship to Jesus, not merely to other people. To be rooted in God, to experience consolation, means to mediate to fellow humans our experience of consolation and contentment. To know this God is to know this God's extended family.

## *Summary of the theology of the psalms of trust or confidence*

1. While life does have its problems, frustrations, and agonies, it also attests to a covenant God who inspires confidence in the midst of these concerns.
2. To pray these psalms to our covenant God also means to pray them for his covenant people, that is, all those who do not experience harmony and equilibrium. Such prayer must be action-oriented.
3. It is not without significance that our ability to trust often emerges after the experience of pain and anxiety.
4. These psalms presuppose a sense of true values. To be hooked on the human quest for power is to destroy the equilibrium and balance assumed by these psalms.
5. These psalms express the radical ability to recall our history with our God and to live trusting lives on the basis of that history.

# CHAPTER 4

# To the Good Life
## The Wisdom Psalms

### *Living versus existing*

Should we merely exist in the expectation of a blessed eternity or dare to live for the sheer joy of living? Is life a burden to be borne with stiff-upper-lip tenacity or is it a gift to be shared with others in community? Is life merely a passage or is it a series of grace-filled moments? Is life to be tolerated or to be lived? Is life to be cursed or to be blessed?

With our great preoccupation with heaven we have been instructed to be dropouts from life. Living thus becomes the condition for the hereafter where accounts will be settled and "genuine" living will begin. We have been taught to put up with life, to make deals with life, so that we may get on with the real business of preparing for our eternal bliss. The heaven symbol has often cheated us out of the possibility of living and thereby out of the opportunity to acknowledge the Living One as the Giver of gifts. With an overemphasis on the beatific vision we can no longer see beatific humans and their gifts.

By and large Israel's wisdom writers (e.g., the authors of Job, Proverbs, and Ecclesiastes) did not accept an afterlife. Their great contribution was to look at life and assess what made for living and what did not. Wisdom was, therefore, the art of steering a course through life, observing both the pluses and minuses. The whole outlook of these writers was based on the gift of creation. In their view God created responsible humans who were to care for their world, not puppets who would mechanically react to the puppeteer's tug of their strings. For these writers humans were charged with the sacred task of transforming God's/their world; they were to relish life because the Creator had proclaimed that it was good, very good.

At prayer we experience the goodness of our God. Our prayers, however, are not to be computer readouts of the qualities of our God. They are not to be layaways for real life later on. At prayer we realize that God is the Giver of gifts and that to acknowledge that gift in any form whatever is to acknowledge the Giver. This does not mean that we fail to see the absence of gifts in so many quarters of our world. Rather, it means that we see the good life as grace for all, not hoarded treasures for only a few. Stability and harmony are to be the heritage of all.

### Wisdom psalms

Wisdom psalms emphasize the doctrine of retribution. Hence they attempt to offer a theological explanation of success and failure, reward and punishment. As a result, they provide black-and-white contrasts between the just and the wicked (see Ps 1:3-4). Wisdom psalms are also bent upon giving sound practical advice. They advocate such virtues as awareness of responsibility, ongoing diligence, and the like (see Ps 37:7-10, 21-22, 34-36). Their hallmark is fear of the Lord (see Ps 112:1), an attitude that is rooted in covenant. To fear the Lord is the basic virtue of religion. It means to respect the person of the Lord and thus be open to the Lord's will and world of concerns.

With regard to stylistic features, wisdom psalms reflect Israel's traditional way of inculcating morality. They offer comparisons: "Better the meagerness of the righteous one / than the plenty of the wicked" (Ps 37:16). They admonish and advise: "Do not be like a horse or mule, without understanding; / with bit and bridle their temper is curbed, / else they will not come to you" (Ps 32:9). They emphasize good living by way of beatitudes: "Blessed is the man to whom the LORD imputes no guilt, / in whose spirit is no deceit" (Ps 32:2). In passing, one should note that there is no clear-cut structure in these psalms.

## Psalm 1
## True Happiness in God's Law

I

¹Blessed is the man who does not walk
    in the counsel of the wicked,
Nor stand in the way of sinners,
    nor sit in company with scoffers.
²Rather, the law of the LORD is his joy;
    and on his law he meditates day and night.
³He is like a tree
    planted near streams of water,
    that yields its fruit in season;
Its leaves never wither;
    whatever he does prospers.

II

⁴But not so are the wicked, not so!
    They are like chaff driven by the wind.
⁵Therefore the wicked will not arise at the judgment,
    nor will sinners in the assembly of the just.
⁶Because the LORD knows the way of the just,
    but the way of the wicked leads to ruin.

Psalm 1 (together with Psalm 2) is really the introduction to the entire book of Psalms. Those responsible for this arrangement have made Psalm 1 provide an attitude that will motivate the entire reading and praying of the subsequent psalms. Thus Psalm 1 is really intended to keep Israel in touch with the Lord, so that the whole book of Psalms is a form of instruction. Taken by itself, Psalm 1 may be prayed as a form of orientation but one that challenges the person at prayer to question the black-and-white picture of orientation that it presents.

This psalm seems to be built around verse 6, that is, the contrast between "the way of the just" and "the way of the wicked." The psalm opens with a beatitude ("Blessed") that implies a certain note of envy. It may be understood as "that person is to be envied who . . ." The psalmist expands the beatitude by dwelling, first of all, on the actions and prosperity of the just. They walk, stand, and sit in the right places (v. 1). Therefore, they may be likened to a channel-fed tree. No matter what, they always get ahead (v. 3). The psalmist then develops the statement of verse 6 by focusing on the wicked. Unlike the just, they will not be able to survive judgment (v. 5). They are comparable to chaff (v. 4), the husks that the wind separates from the grain.

The study of God's law fills out the description of the just. They are rooted in a person, the Lord, and they are moved to carry out the wise instruction ("law") of the Lord. To separate the person of God from the will of God is always a distortion.

At prayer we may feel inclined to interpret the Lord's rewards and punishments in terms of an afterlife. Thus in heaven the just will be rewarded while the wicked will be condemned in hell. However, the perspective of the psalmist is this-worldly; reward and punishment occur in this life. In our now halting effort at prayer we may be able to think of some of those genuine people who "made it in this life." Nonetheless we continue to be haunted by the specter of the wicked who also "made it in this life." In the end we may have to be content with a gray world, not the black-and-white world of this psalm.

Order, normalcy, equilibrium—this is the picture of the psalmist wherein the channel-fed tree and the wind-blown chaff are clearly distinguished. But our experience faults this picture. We feel like the author of Job who must challenge the divine judge: "Oh, that I had one to hear my case" (Job 31:35). Perhaps the challenge of the psalm is to accept the presence of mystery. Like Job we are invited, not to turn aside from harsh reality and fail to make our contribution, but to place the demands for order, normalcy, and equilibrium in a Person, not a system. For us this may prove to be the law or wise instruction of the psalm: to be in touch with our God, not to be caught up in programs. Thus we are challenged to question the doctrine of rewards and punishments but yet accept the wise instruction, difficult though it may be. At prayer we are in the company of the wise who sought to steer a way through life.

## Psalm 112
### The Blessings of the Just

¹Hallelujah!
Blessed the man who fears the LORD,
    who greatly delights in his commands.

²His descendants shall be mighty in the land,
    a generation of the upright will be blessed.
³Wealth and riches shall be in his house;
    his righteousness shall endure forever.
⁴Light shines through the darkness for the upright;
    gracious, compassionate, and righteous.
⁵It is good for the man gracious in lending,
    who conducts his affairs with justice.
⁶For he shall never be shaken;
    the righteous shall be remembered forever.
⁷He shall not fear an ill report;
    his heart is steadfast, trusting the LORD.
⁸His heart is tranquil, without fear,
    till at last he looks down on his foes.
⁹Lavishly he gives to the poor;
    his righteousness shall endure forever;
    his horn shall be exalted in honor.
¹⁰The wicked sees and is angry;
    gnashes his teeth and wastes away;
    the desire of the wicked comes to nothing.

This psalm is an acrostic (see Ps 145), that is, a composition in which the initial letters form a pattern—here the letters of the Hebrew alphabet. Although this may seem somewhat artificial, the psalmist has artistically constructed a poem that, like Psalm 1, contrasts the behavior of the righteous and the wicked. Like the author of Psalm 1, this poet also begins with a beatitude (v. 1) and builds his composition around a contrasting proverb: the righteousness of the just endures forever (vv. 3, 6, 9) while the desires of the wicked are frustrated.

In verses 2-3 the psalmist notes the blessings of the righteous: prosperity and family. In verses 4-6 he depicts the proper behavior of the righteous: generosity and honesty. In verses 7-9 he underlines the faith of the righteous: deep trust, tranquillity, concern for the poor, and honor ("horn" in v. 9 is an image for increased dignity and strength; see Pss 75:11; 89:18). Finally in verse 10 he focuses on the state of the wicked: jealous rage and anger occasioned by the stature and good fortune of the righteous. The psalm concludes with the sage remark that the desires of the wicked lead only to frustration.

For the righteous, life is indeed worth living. It is a good life replete with family and wealth. It is a life devoid of shocks and preoccupations. It is a life where the good will indeed have the last word. Clearly the basis of this life is fear of the Lord and delight in his commandments (v. 1). It is an understatement to say that this is a world of harmony and balance.

As in Psalm 1, we are tempted at prayer to shift this world of bliss to the afterlife. However, the only measure of immortality allotted to the righteous in this psalm is the preservation of their virtue in the ongoing memory of the community. Still, while our experience conflicts with this picture, we are challenged at prayer to make at least some elements in this outlook viable. We are urged to repress evil and to honor virtue in our lives and our community's life. In this way we are called upon to discover the good and unmask the evil. Even though our world will never resemble a perfect world, at prayer we are moved to make it more livable so that the righteous may be duly acknowledged and the wicked exposed and rehabilitated. To contribute a little to the order of our world is to overcome some of its disorder.

## Psalm 128
## The Blessed Home of the Just

¹A song of ascents.

I

Blessed are all who fear the Lord,
    and who walk in his ways.
²What your hands provide you will enjoy;
    you will be blessed and prosper:
³Your wife will be like a fruitful vine
    within your home,
Your children like young olive plants
    around your table.
⁴Just so will the man be blessed
    who fears the Lord.

II
⁵May the LORD bless you from Zion;
    may you see Jerusalem's prosperity
    all the days of your life,
      ⁶and live to see your children's children.
Peace upon Israel!

Like the two previous psalms, this psalm also begins with a beatitude. In the opening verse fearing the Lord is equated with walking in his ways. In the following verses the psalmist develops the consequences of such a way of life. According to verse 2 such people will know prosperity, that is, they will enjoy what they have worked for. According to verse 3 the wife will be fertile and thus have a large family. Verse 4 emphasizes this desirable situation by noting the dimension of blessing. Thus, to fear the Lord = to walk in his ways = to be blessed.

This psalm is similar to the Aaronic blessing (see Num 6:22-26) in its emphasis on peace and blessings. It is highly significant here that the blessing of those fearing the Lord in verses 1-4 is linked to the prosperity of Jerusalem (v. 5). In the psalmist's view the individual and the community are not two isolated entities. They mutually interact so that the success of one redounds to that of the other. The pilgrim worshiping at the Jerusalem temple is both member of a people and member of a household.

This temple-home theology overlaps with the dimension of harmony and balance typical of the wisdom psalms. First, blessing is a bridge that moves from the sanctuary to the ongoing life of the community outside the sanctuary. Second, the frame of reference is divine providence whereby God continues to care for his people. Third, God's blessing is located in continuity, not a few extraordinary events.

At prayer we are urged to dwell on the ongoing dimension of life, not a few extraordinary events. Hence a good job, a good spouse, a lovely family, and grandchildren make for that wholeness wherein living becomes celebration. To be sure, this psalm does not deal with unemployment, marital crisis, problems in raising children, and so forth. And yet by reason of blessing itself these issues emerge. To participate in the community's worship is to be involved in the community's destiny. One's personal life is thus bound up with Jerusalem. To acknowledge the harmony and balance in our own lives means to be aware of the disharmony and imbalance in the lives of others. God's family is present when we are at the seemingly most intimate moments of our prayer.

## Psalm 127
## The Need of God's Blessing

¹A song of ascents. Of Solomon.

I

Unless the LORD build the house,
    they labor in vain who build.
Unless the LORD guard the city,
    in vain does the guard keep watch.
²It is vain for you to rise early
    and put off your rest at night,
To eat bread earned by hard toil—
    all this God gives to his beloved in sleep.

II

³Certainly sons are a gift from the LORD,
    the fruit of the womb, a reward.
⁴Like arrows in the hand of a warrior
    are the sons born in one's youth.
⁵Blessed is the man who has filled his quiver with them.
He will never be shamed
    for he will destroy his foes at the gate.

This psalm consists of two extended wisdom sayings: (1) verses 1-2 and (2) verses 3-5. The first saying underlines the futility of human effort apart from the Lord's active involvement. The second saying emphasizes the blessing of many children. Together both sayings teach that human prosperity is not the product of sustained human activity but God's gift. The word "house" in verse 1 is linked to the large family in verses 3-5. "House" can mean temple, royal palace, dynasty, or family. Since this psalm is a song of ascents and thus occurs during a pilgrimage to the City of David (see Ps 121), the "house" and the "city" of verse 1 are the temple and Jerusalem respectively (see Ps 122:1, 5). The family is also a "house": to found a family is "to build a house." "House" unites both parts of the psalm, emphasizing God's gift-giving in all segments of Israel's life.

While this psalm does not reject human effort outright, it clearly insists on the primacy of God's generosity. In verse 2 the psalmist captures this aspect: "all this God *gives* to his beloved in sleep" (emphasis added). In verse 4 the notion of giving reappears when the psalmist remarks that children are also the Lord's gift (note the use of the verb "to give" in Eccl 1:13; 5:17; 12:7). Given the infant mortality rate in the ancient Near East, children were highly prized, especially sons (see Job 3:3; Jer 20:15). Indeed the more adult sons a man had, the more influential he would be "at the gate" (v. 5), that is, in the legal disputes that were settled there (see Prov 31:23).

Prayer, like most of human life, involves a tension—here a tension between human effort and divine gift. This psalm reminds us that despite our American heritage, autonomy in itself is not the greatest value. We are urged to explore our successes and our achievements against the background of the Lord's generosity. At prayer we must admit that we are also beneficiaries of a gift-giving God.

## Psalm 32
## Remission of Sin

<sup>1</sup>Of David. A *maskil*.

I

Blessed is the one whose fault is removed,
    whose sin is forgiven.
<sup>2</sup>Blessed is the man to whom the LORD imputes no guilt,
    in whose spirit is no deceit.

II

<sup>3</sup>Because I kept silent, my bones wasted away;
    I groaned all day long.
<sup>4</sup>For day and night your hand was heavy upon me;
    my strength withered as in dry summer heat.

*Selah*

<sup>5</sup>Then I declared my sin to you;
    my guilt I did not hide.
I said, "I confess my transgression to the LORD,"
    and you took away the guilt of my sin.

*Selah*

⁶Therefore every loyal person should pray to you
>    in time of distress.
Though flood waters threaten,
>    they will never reach him.
⁷You are my shelter; you guard me from distress;
>    with joyful shouts of deliverance you surround me.

>                                                        *Selah*

III
⁸I will instruct you and show you the way you should walk,
>    give you counsel with my eye upon you.
⁹Do not be like a horse or mule, without understanding;
>    with bit and bridle their temper is curbed,
>    else they will not come to you.
IV
¹⁰Many are the sorrows of the wicked one,
>    but mercy surrounds the one who trusts in the LORD.
¹¹Be glad in the LORD and rejoice, you righteous;
>    exult, all you upright of heart.

This psalm is one of the so-called seven penitential psalms (see Pss 6; 38; 51; 102; 130; 143). This title dates from the seventh century AD and is applied to those psalms that are very apt for expressing repentance. All such psalms capture intense moments in the relationship between the Lord and Israel. (A "maskil" may mean something like a contemplative or didactic poem.)

The psalm opens (vv. 1-2) with the statement that the forgiven are truly happy or blessed. The psalmist observes that for the good life nothing quite matches the experience of forgiveness. Once this God has acted, there is no imputation of any continuing guilt (v. 2). In verses 3-7 the psalmist shares his story of sin and reconciliation. He describes the weight, the burden of unacknowledged wrongdoing (vv. 3-4). He then reports his declaration of sin (v. 5) and his subsequent release and liberation from this danger ("flood waters") that overwhelmed him (vv. 6-7). In verses 8-11 the psalmist resumes his teaching role, warning the listener not to be stubborn like the animals. Fittingly the just and upright of heart are invited to share in the great joy of the author.

This is a marvelous study of the psychology of sin and forgiveness. Unacknowledged sin has a profound impact on the total person: bones wasting away, groaning all day long, strength withering (v. 4). The psalmist further notes that there is no hesitation or delay between confession and forgiveness (v. 5). It is the psalmist's expressed confession of sin that breaks the silence of despair (v. 3). To articulate one's guilt is to open oneself up to liberation and well-being. Only sincere speech effects the alleviation of pain.

At prayer we may choose to recall our reconciliation with our God as well as with our sisters and brothers. We may elect to remember the effort required to say to someone we had offended, "I ask your forgiveness." We may further opt to recall that sensation of at-oneness when the offended person replied, "I forgive you." Acknowledgment of sin makes possible the restoration of human relationships. Ultimately, "I forgive you" is but another way of saying, "I love you."

The covenant dimension of prayer may demand that we, the offended party, initiate this whole process of reconciliation. Hence we may be required to offer forgiveness before even being approached. To the extent that we can overcome the flood waters (v. 6) of hurt and contempt, we imitate the God of Psalm 32 who is shelter, keeps the sinner from distress, and rings him or her round with safety (v. 7). Ours is the awesome responsibility to restore wasted bones and withered strength. The God of this psalm calls for more practitioners of such restoration in daily life where hurt and rejection are all too common. The reconciling person is the truly free person since he or she experiences liberation from the shackles of ego.

## Psalm 34
### Thanksgiving to God Who Delivers the Just

¹Of David, when he feigned madness before Abimelech, who drove him out and he went away.

I

²I will bless the LORD at all times;
　his praise shall be always in my mouth.
³My soul will glory in the LORD;
　let the poor hear and be glad.

⁴Magnify the LORD with me;
  and let us exalt his name together.

II

⁵I sought the LORD, and he answered me,
  delivered me from all my fears.
⁶Look to him and be radiant,
  and your faces may not blush for shame.
⁷This poor one cried out and the LORD heard,
  and from all his distress he saved him.
⁸The angel of the LORD encamps
  around those who fear him, and he saves them.
⁹Taste and see that the LORD is good;
  blessed is the stalwart one who takes refuge in him.
¹⁰Fear the LORD, you his holy ones;
  nothing is lacking to those who fear him.
¹¹The rich grow poor and go hungry,
  but those who seek the LORD lack no good thing.

III

¹²Come, children, listen to me;
  I will teach you fear of the LORD.
¹³Who is the man who delights in life,
  who loves to see the good days?
¹⁴Keep your tongue from evil,
  your lips from speaking lies.
¹⁵Turn from evil and do good;
  seek peace and pursue it.
¹⁶The eyes of the LORD are directed toward the righteous
  and his ears toward their cry.
¹⁷The LORD's face is against evildoers
  to wipe out their memory from the earth.
¹⁸The righteous cry out, the LORD hears
  and he rescues them from all their afflictions.
¹⁹The LORD is close to the brokenhearted,
  saves those whose spirit is crushed.
²⁰Many are the troubles of the righteous,
  but the LORD delivers him from them all.
²¹He watches over all his bones;
  not one of them shall be broken.

²²Evil will slay the wicked;
  those who hate the righteous are condemned.
²³The LORD is the redeemer of the souls of his servants;
  and none are condemned who take refuge in him.

In this psalm (also an acrostic) the poet announces in his introduction his intention to praise the Lord (vv. 2-4), noting in verse 3 that the poor may derive profit from his action. In verses 5-11 the psalmist sees his experience, not as an isolated incident, but as one that necessarily impacts the whole community. The God of Israel is involved in the plight of individuals. However, the deliverance is reenacted and celebrated so that others may benefit from what would otherwise be a one-time event. In verse 8 the poet uses the image of the angel of the Lord. This is basically another form of the Lord's presence whereby the God of the covenant protects his people (see Exod 3:2, 4; 14:19-20). Though the powerful may experience poverty and hunger, those who fear the Lord suffer no want (v. 11).

In verses 12-13 the psalmist applies his experience to the needs of his audience. As he sees it, wisdom is a question of loving life and enjoying good days (v. 13). To acquire such gifts, one must control one's speech (v. 14) and avoid evil/do good (v. 15). By practicing righteousness, the wise integrate themselves into the divinely willed flow of the world. Should they fall into distress, they are able to call upon the Lord and find relief (vv. 18-21). On the other hand, the wicked are necessarily bent upon disrupting the community and causing havoc. It is only fitting that they be removed from the community—hence their memory is obliterated (v. 17). Evil will eventually wipe out evil.

At prayer we must also recall the disruptive experiences in our lives. We are to recollect the times when for one reason or another order gave way to disorder, balance ceded to imbalance, and harmony yielded to disharmony. We are thus bidden to attempt to heal a broken world, a world where wisdom is obviously lacking, a world where life and peace are only trite expressions. However, our prayer is not to be an exercise in recalling old falls and catastrophes for memory's sake. Rather, our prayer must make our experience contagious for those who exist but really do not live. Prayer must touch the broken community in which we find ourselves so that our experience may be the springboard for hope that is the condition for life. At prayer we are to become the embodiment of the God who "watches over all his bones; / not one of them shall be broken" (v. 21). Respect ("fear") for the person of the Lord compels us to act on behalf of the hurting.

## Psalm 37
## The Fate of Sinners and the Reward of the Just

[1]Of David.
Aleph
Do not be provoked by evildoers;
    do not envy those who do wrong.
[2]Like grass they wither quickly;
    like green plants they wilt away.

Beth
[3]Trust in the LORD and do good
    that you may dwell in the land and live secure.
[4]Find your delight in the LORD
    who will give you your heart's desire.

Gimel
[5]Commit your way to the LORD;
    trust in him and he will act
[6]And make your righteousness shine like the dawn,
    your justice like noonday.

Daleth
[7]Be still before the LORD;
    wait for him.
Do not be provoked by the prosperous,
    nor by malicious schemers.

He
[8]Refrain from anger; abandon wrath;
    do not be provoked; it brings only harm.
[9]Those who do evil will be cut off,
    but those who wait for the LORD will inherit the earth.

Waw
[10]Wait a little, and the wicked will be no more;
    look for them and they will not be there.
[11]But the poor will inherit the earth,
    will delight in great prosperity.

Zayin

[12]The wicked plot against the righteous
and gnash their teeth at them;
[13]But my Lord laughs at them,
because he sees that their day is coming.

Heth

[14]The wicked unsheath their swords;
they string their bows
To fell the poor and oppressed,
to slaughter those whose way is upright.
[15]Their swords will pierce their own hearts;
their bows will be broken.

Teth

[16]Better the meagerness of the righteous one
than the plenty of the wicked.
[17]The arms of the wicked will be broken,
while the LORD will sustain the righteous.

Yodh

[18]The LORD knows the days of the blameless;
their heritage lasts forever.
[19]They will not be ashamed when times are bad;
in days of famine they will be satisfied.

Kaph

[20]The wicked perish,
enemies of the LORD;
They shall be consumed like fattened lambs;
like smoke they disappear.

Lamedh

[21]The wicked one borrows but does not repay;
the righteous one is generous and gives.
[22]For those blessed by the Lord will inherit the earth,
but those accursed will be cut off.

Mem

[23]The valiant one whose steps are guided by the LORD,
who will delight in his way,
[24]May stumble, but he will never fall,
for the LORD holds his hand.

Nun

²⁵Neither in my youth, nor now in old age
    have I seen the righteous one abandoned
    or his offspring begging for bread.
²⁶All day long he is gracious and lends,
    and his offspring become a blessing.

Samekh

²⁷Turn from evil and do good,
    that you may be settled forever.
²⁸For the LORD loves justice
    and does not abandon the faithful.

Ayin

When the unjust are destroyed,
    and the offspring of the wicked cut off,
²⁹The righteous will inherit the earth
    and dwell in it forever.

Pe

³⁰The mouth of the righteous utters wisdom;
    his tongue speaks what is right.
³¹God's teaching is in his heart;
    his steps do not falter.

Sadhe

³²The wicked spies on the righteous
    and seeks to kill him.
³³But the LORD does not abandon him in his power,
    nor let him be condemned when tried.

Qoph

³⁴Wait eagerly for the LORD,
    and keep his way;
He will raise you up to inherit the earth;
    you will see when the wicked are cut off.

Resh

³⁵I have seen a ruthless scoundrel,
    spreading out like a green cedar.
³⁶When I passed by again, he was gone;
    though I searched, he could not be found.

Shin

<sup>37</sup>Observe the person of integrity and mark the upright;
　　Because there is a future for a man of peace.
<sup>38</sup>Sinners will be destroyed together;
　　the future of the wicked will be cut off.

Taw

<sup>39</sup>The salvation of the righteous is from the LORD,
　　their refuge in a time of distress.
<sup>40</sup>The LORD helps and rescues them,
　　rescues and saves them from the wicked,
　　because they take refuge in him.

This psalm is an acrostic in which the letters of the Hebrew alphabet are actually mentioned and serve to introduce two-verse sections. The author presents himself as an older sage (vv. 25, 35-36) who recognizes the problem of social justice faced by his younger audience (v. 7).

The psalmist begins his handling of the social justice issue by mentioning the evildoers who will not have the final word (vv. 1-2). In advocating trust, the sage proclaims that trusting and doing good will lead to dwelling in the land and enjoying security (v. 3). In verse 6 he assures his audience that God will make their "righteousness shine like the dawn" and their "justice like noonday." In verse 9 he distinguishes between the fate of the just and the unjust. While evildoers will be cut off, those waiting for the Lord will inherit the land. The land motif reappears in verse 11, where the poor are promised great prosperity in addition to inheriting the earth. Verse 12 vividly portrays the plotting of the wicked against the righteous by noting the gnashing of teeth. In verse 22 the blessed and the accursed are distinguished. The former will inherit the earth while the latter will be cut off. Finally in verse 29 the poet adds that the righteous will dwell in the land forever.

In view of heinous violations of human justice the sage offers timely advice. He emphasizes that the Lord is not immune to or oblivious of such violations. The God of Israel is indeed committed to his covenant partner. According to verse 3 the proper reaction of this partner is trust in the Lord. Furthermore, the Lord will not abandon the righteous to the power of the unrighteous nor will he pronounce the just guilty at the time of trial. On the other hand, the socially oppressed should not take matters into their own hands. They are to curb their anger since it will only lead to harm (v. 8).

In verses 37-38 the author develops the notion of time with regard to the righteous and the unrighteous. Since God's rewarding and punishing occur only on earth, the "future" (v. 37) is very important. This future includes all of one's hopes, for example, longevity, descendants, prosperity, well-being, and so on. According to the psalmist only the righteous will have a future since the wicked will be utterly cut off.

At prayer we must not allow ourselves to be lulled into complacency by focusing merely on the needs of our tiny world. Prayer is that occasion when we concern ourselves with the shocks and atrocities noted in our news media. Covenant will not permit us to tune out the cries of the socially oppressed. Where there is social oppression, there is disorder. And where there is disorder, there is a situation that the wise cannot tolerate. Prayer must move us into the future of the psalmist so that pain will be redressed now and the land will be returned now. Prayer and social justice go hand in hand. To pray this psalm and then to neglect social justice is not to pray at all.

## Psalm 49
## Confidence in God Rather than in Riches

¹For the leader. A psalm of the Korahites.
²Hear this, all you peoples!
    Give ear, all who inhabit the world,
³You of lowly birth or high estate,
    rich and poor together.
⁴My mouth shall speak words of wisdom,
    my heart shall offer insights.
⁵I will turn my ear to a riddle,
    expound my question on a lyre.

I
⁶Why should I fear in evil days,
    with the iniquity of my assailants surrounding me,
⁷Of those who trust in their wealth
    and boast of their abundant riches?
⁸No man can ransom even a brother,
    or pay to God his own ransom.

⁹The redemption of his soul is costly;
   and he will pass away forever.
¹⁰Will he live on forever, then,
   and never see the Pit of Corruption?
¹¹Indeed, he will see that the wise die,
   and the fool will perish together with the senseless,
   and they leave their wealth to others.
¹²Their tombs are their homes forever,
   their dwellings through all generations,
"They named countries after themselves"
   ¹³—but man does not abide in splendor.
   He is like the beasts—they perish.

II

¹⁴This is the way of those who trust in themselves,
   and the end of those who take pleasure in their own mouth.
                                                                        *Selah*

¹⁵Like a herd of sheep they will be put into Sheol,
   and Death will shepherd them.
Straight to the grave they descend,
   where their form will waste away,
   Sheol will be their palace.
¹⁶But God will redeem my life,
   will take me from the hand of Sheol.

                                                                        *Selah*

¹⁷Do not fear when a man becomes rich,
   when the wealth of his house grows great.
¹⁸At his death he will not take along anything,
   his glory will not go down after him.
¹⁹During his life his soul uttered blessings;
   "They will praise you, for you do well for yourself."
²⁰But he will join the company of his fathers,
   never again to see the light.
²¹In his prime, man does not understand.
   He is like the beasts—they perish.

This wisdom psalm addresses the perennial problem of the success and
prosperity of the wicked. (The Korahites of v. 1 were members of Le-
vitical guilds who as singers performed service in the temple during the

postexilic period.) However, in the face of the apparent advantage of unjust wealth this psalm affirms confidence in God. In the opening section (vv. 2-5) the psalmist invites the community to ponder this "riddle" and "question" (v. 5). These terms imply that it is not a question of obvious common sense. But in considering the question, the poet shrewdly reaches out to both rich and poor alike (v. 3), implying that they are actually equal. The psalmist then describes the self-delusion of the wealthy whose fate is to die like ignorant beasts (vv. 6-13). Finally the writer teaches that the wealth of the unjust should not cause difficulties, for God will intervene and save the just (vv. 14-21).

This psalm presupposes a false reading of reality, namely, that wealth and poverty are the criteria of value. One senses that the psalmist speaks to the concern of those who resent the injustice of virtue having no reward. The response of the psalmist to this concern is to assert that death is the great equalizer and hence the wealthy really do not enjoy any advantage. To the question of fear (v. 6) the psalmist answers that there are no grounds for fear (v. 17). Connected with the rejection of fear is the clear statement that no one can save his or her life (vv. 9-10)—one cannot buy one's way out of death. After all, "you can't take it with you" (see v. 18). By way of contrast, however, God can buy back ("redeem") those who trust in him, not wealth (v. 16). This is not an appeal for an afterlife but an article of faith that God will not reject the vulnerable poor.

At prayer we must not deny that we are participants in an exceedingly consumeristic society. Our tendency is to place enormous value on things. In addition, we are tempted to give greater honor and esteem to those "who have made it." While we must not disparage those who have acquired their wealth justly, we must ask ourselves this lingering question: What determines our sense of values? This psalm suggests that there is a God who bids us to trust and, in trusting, to rearrange our priorities.

Perhaps we suffer a greater distortion as we attempt to read this psalm today. Whereas the psalmist and his audience rejected belief in an afterlife, we may be tempted to exploit our acceptance of an afterlife unjustly. Thus we may be naive enough to leave the resolution of injustices and inequities to the final judgment, to the option of either eternal bliss or eternal punishment. At prayer we are called to be activists as well. We prepare for the "good" life of heaven only by bettering the lot of our sisters and brothers in this less than perfect life.

## New Testament

### Luke 6:20-21

[20]And raising his eyes toward his disciples he said:
"Blessed are you who are poor,
    for the kingdom of God is yours.
[21]Blessed are you who are now hungry,
    for you will be satisfied.
Blessed are you who are now weeping,
    for you will laugh."

The historical Jesus probably pronounced these beatitudes in the third person ("Blessed are the poor, for theirs is the kingdom of God"). As such, they correspond to the formulation of the wisdom psalms. Against the background of his biblical tradition, Jesus sees himself as a wise person, one bent upon offering a guide for steering through life. These beatitudes may be understood, therefore, as Jesus' plan for harmony, balance, and equilibrium in his Father's kingdom. They speak to that situation where existence will become celebration because all needs will be met. Jesus' ministry is the occasion for pronouncing the poor, the hungry, and the weeping blessed because he has set out to reverse their lot. Jesus' audience is not deemed blessed because of their spiritual qualities but because of God's action in Jesus.

In his inaugural sermon in the Nazareth synagogue (Luke 4:16-30), Luke has Jesus outline his ministry in terms of Isaiah 58:6; 61:1-2: "The Spirit of the Lord is upon me, / because he has anointed me / to bring glad tidings to the poor. / He has sent me to proclaim liberty to captives / and recovery of sight to the blind, / to let the oppressed go free, / and to proclaim a year acceptable to the Lord" (Luke 4:18-19). For Luke this sermon provides the substance of the preaching of Jesus. Against the background of the beatitudes Jesus is once more the wise person who announces the end of disharmony and disillusionment and the start of harmony and hope. Jesus' mission concerns the unfortunate. He solemnly announces that their suffering has ended. What is significant is that Jesus understands the restoration of God's order as linked to his own person. In him the wisdom psalms take on a deeper meaning.

In both Matthew and Luke, Jesus dispels the doubts of John the Baptist concerning his Father's plans (see Matt 11:2-6; Luke 7:18-23).

Those plans are not the fire and brimstone envisioned by John (see Matt 3:11-12; Luke 3:16-17). They are, rather, healing of the blind, the cripples, the lepers, and the deaf, as well as raising the dead and preaching the Good News to the poor. John was scandalized by Jesus' sense of mission. In correcting John's view, Jesus utters a beatitude: "And blessed is the one who takes no offense at me" (Matt 11:6; Luke 7:23). For Jesus, his mission consists in overcoming all those obstacles that make living less than celebration. In Jesus' world a fully human life is a gift to be cherished in community, not a down payment to be honored in the heavenly banking house.

The New Testament's teaching on Eucharist and the role of wisdom are significant for daily living. In the book of Proverbs, wisdom is personified as God's unique creature. She beckons to humans to accept God's view of reality and act accordingly: "Does not Wisdom call, / and Understanding raise her voice? / On the top of the heights along the road, / at the crossroads she takes her stand" (Prov 8:1-2). Having built her house, Lady Wisdom invites the wise to partake of her table: "Come, eat of my food, / and drink of the wine I have mixed!" (Prov 9:5). In Eucharist the exhortations and teachings of Jesus, God's unique sage, are set against the background of bread and wine. To partake of the bread and the cup is to share the worldview of this sage. To be welcomed to this table means to translate that wisdom into action whereby our distorted world becomes less chaotic and disorganized. To share Eucharist is to imbibe a wisdom whereby the participants become bread and wine for others. Eucharist means "the good life" only insofar as other humans are made whole and thus rendered capable of celebrating, not just tolerating, life.

## *Summary of the theology of the wisdom psalms*

1. Harmony, order, and balance are to be reflected not only in the universe but also in the lives of fellow humans.
2. Wisdom, the plan for achieving this equilibrium, is rooted in a person, the Lord, and in respect for and openness to the Lord's plan, that is, fear of the Lord.
3. Genuine human life is one in which celebration is paramount. Life is not merely a passage or a condition for making it in the hereafter. Life is a gift from the Creator to be shared in community.

4. True wisdom is not an ego trip. To have a good life also means to better the lives of others. To be happy is to make others happy.

5. Although the formulation "righteousness equals success, wickedness equals failure" is faulted by our experience, wisdom recommends that we seek to extol goodness and denounce evil in this life.

# CHAPTER 5

# Prayers for the Institution
## The Royal Psalms

*Personal versus communal good*

Ideally, at least, political officeholders envision the common good, not personal gain. Frequently, however, the politician is not the one who realizes the expectations of the community. Somehow we have come to accept as a fact of life that new titles and new offices can mean the enhancement of the holder, not the improvement of the people. Nonetheless to be leader means to exist for others. As a result, the community has a right to expect a reasonable quality of performance.

The temptation to exploit power is not limited to high government officials. We observe it in our own families and local communities. The bearer of a title, for example, husband, wife, father, or mother, may manipulate another or others out of purely selfish interests. Perhaps one of our greatest challenges is the mature use of the power conferred on us by our family position, job, or society at large. Indeed no one is free from the self-serving drive of power, not even our church and its officials. In 5:29-30 Matthew has Jesus forbidding sexual lust in an individual. However, in 18:8-9 he has Jesus prohibiting lust for power in the church.

In the understanding of the ancient Near East, the king held a sacred position between the gods and the people. The king functioned as a steward of the gods, representing them on earth. It was through the king that the gods exercised their power, so that through him the blessings of fertility flowed to the people. The king also represented the people before the gods. Indeed he was the very incorporation of the people. Consequently the people shared the strength and blessing that the king received from the gods.

According to the traditions in 1 Samuel 7–15 kingship did not emerge easily in Israel. Political realities, such as the Philistine oppression, made it a necessity. While Israel, however, could not accept the pagan implications of kingship in the ancient Near East, God's people could in part understand the king as the mediator between the Lord and the people. Ideally, "Long live the king!" meant "Long live the people!"

At prayer we cannot avoid the implications of our own royalty. According to the opening chapters of Genesis, God freely chooses to run the risk of monarchy. God makes men and women kings and queens so that they may be instruments of his concern for others (see Gen 1:27-28; 2:6-7). Hence in praying these psalms, we too are addressed. We are invited not only to sense the headiness of our royal prerogatives but also to test the reality of our royal accomplishments. At prayer we are asked whether we have made our contribution to the harmony, peace, and equilibrium of our royal domain. Thus prayer is the dangerous rendezvous for reflecting on the reality of our obligations, not our rights. The royal psalms remind us forcefully that to have power means to empower others to a genuinely human life.

### Royal psalms

The royal psalms are prayers related to the Davidic dynasty, that is, the line of kings descended from King David. They are distinguished more by content than by literary characteristics. Hence they have no special structure. For example, Psalms 2, 21, 72, 101, and 110 celebrate the king's coronation or its anniversary. Psalm 45 is a poem for a royal wedding. Psalm 20 is a prayer for the king's victory in time of war. It is worth noting that not all royal psalms fit under orientation. For example, Psalm 18 is a thanksgiving or psalm of declarative praise while Psalm 89 is a communal lament. Moreover, these royal psalms do not refer to a specific Davidic king. Rather, they celebrate the ideal king. In this sense one may speak of them as prayers for the institution.

According to the theology of these psalms the king is the Lord's "messiah" (derived from the Hebrew word meaning "anointed"; it is translated into Greek as "christ"). As such, the king is the instrument of God's concern for the people. In keeping with the view of the ancient Near East, the king is the incorporation of his people. He is also the Lord's adopted son. Every Davidic king has the right to lay claim to this divine pronouncement: "I will be a father to him [the Davidic king], and he shall be a son to me. If he does wrong, I will reprove him with a human rod and with human punishments; but I will not withdraw my favor from him" (2 Sam 7:14-15). It is remarkable that Israel continued to pray these psalms after the sixth century BC when there was no longer a Davidic king. By persevering in this practice and by making Psalm 2 (along with Psalm 1) the introduction to the book of Psalms, Israel entertained the hope that eventually there would be another royal presence in their midst.

## Psalm 132
## The Covenant Between David and God

¹A song of ascents.

I

Remember, O LORD, for David
    all his hardships;
²How he swore an oath to the LORD,
    vowed to the Mighty One of Jacob:
³"I will not enter the house where I live,
    nor lie on the couch where I sleep;
⁴I will give my eyes no sleep,
    my eyelids no rest,
⁵Till I find a place for the LORD,
    a dwelling for the Mighty One of Jacob."
⁶"We have heard of it in Ephrathah;
    we have found it in the fields of Jaar.
⁷Let us enter his dwelling;
    let us worship at his footstool."
⁸"Arise, LORD, come to your resting place,
    you and your mighty ark.

⁹"Your priests will be clothed with justice;
  your devout will shout for joy."
¹⁰For the sake of David your servant,
  do not reject your anointed.

II

¹¹The LORD swore an oath to David in truth,
  he will never turn back from it:
"Your own offspring I will set upon your throne.
¹²If your sons observe my covenant,
  and my decrees I shall teach them,
Their sons, in turn,
  shall sit forever on your throne."
¹³Yes, the LORD has chosen Zion,
  desired it for a dwelling:
¹⁴"This is my resting place forever;
  here I will dwell, for I desire it.
¹⁵I will bless Zion with provisions;
  its poor I will fill with bread.
¹⁶I will clothe its priests with salvation;
  its devout shall shout for joy.
¹⁷There I will make a horn sprout for David;
  I will set a lamp for my anointed.
¹⁸His foes I will clothe with shame,
  but on him his crown shall shine."

This royal psalm is a liturgy commemorating the Lord's covenant with David and his choice of Zion. However, it is not clear on which precise feast this liturgy was celebrated. It may be divided as follows: (1) a prayer for David because of his great concern for the Lord's dwelling place (vv. 1-5; probably a priest or some cultic official read this prayer); (2) the ritual of the processional bearing of the ark (a portable box or chest that symbolized the Lord's throne in the temple) into Jerusalem (vv. 6-10) in which the choir would recite the story of David's discovery of the ark (2 Sam 6); (3) the Lord's promise of an eternal (though conditional) dynasty (vv. 11-12); (4) the Lord's everlasting choice of Zion (vv. 13-18).

In the first section the psalmist exaggerates David's preoccupation with the ark by creating an oath whereby David will not sleep until the ark is found. Unlike the story in 2 Samuel 6:1-15, Psalm 132 presupposes that the location of the ark is not known. When, however, it is discovered, the choir takes up the old battle cry (see Num 10:35-36), asking that the Lord now move from his present dwelling place to his new one in Jerusalem (v. 8). The transfer becomes the occasion for appealing for victory on behalf of the priests and the faithful (v. 9) as well as the Davidic king (v. 10).

In the third section the psalmist speaks of the Lord's oath to David (v. 11) as conditional, not absolute: "*If* your sons observe my covenant" (v. 12; emphasis added). Hence David and his line are not absolute monarchs—they are answerable to the Lord and, in turn, to the needs of the people. In the final section the Lord's possession of his new resting place means the fulfillment of the petitions in verses 9-10. After mentioning the Lord's provision for the poor, the priests, and the faithful (vv. 15-16), the psalmist directs most of his attention to David. Thus David will have descendants (v. 17: "make a horn sprout for David"). He will also experience security and divine presence (v. 17: "a lamp for my anointed"). He will see, moreover, the downfall of his enemies and the glory of his own reign (v. 18).

At prayer we cannot help but be overwhelmed by the interaction of human effort and divine grace in this psalm. To David's oath to find the ark there corresponds the Lord's oath to create the Davidic dynasty. There is here a dimension of intimacy that we must relish but an intimacy that is linked to obedience to the God of this covenant. In anticipating the honors and grandeur of royalty, we must also bear in mind the condition attached to them, namely, obedience to the Lord's covenant and decrees (v. 12). To be treated as kings and queens means that we have upheld and promoted the royal character of our fellow humans. It is only intimacy translated into obedience that creates the kingdom where order, stability, and equilibrium reign. At prayer we are reminded that the only fitting royal emblem is service to others.

### Psalm 2
### A Psalm for a Royal Coronation

¹Why do the nations protest
    and the peoples conspire in vain?
²Kings on earth rise up
    and princes plot together
        against the LORD and against his anointed one:

³"Let us break their shackles
   and cast off their chains from us!"
⁴The one enthroned in heaven laughs;
   the Lord derides them,
⁵Then he speaks to them in his anger,
   in his wrath he terrifies them:
⁶"I myself have installed my king
   on Zion, my holy mountain."
⁷I will proclaim the decree of the LORD,
   he said to me, "You are my son;
   today I have begotten you.
⁸Ask it of me,
   and I will give you the nations as your inheritance,
   and, as your possession, the ends of the earth.
⁹With an iron rod you will shepherd them,
   like a potter's vessel you will shatter them."
¹⁰And now, kings, give heed;
   take warning, judges on earth.
¹¹Serve the LORD with fear;
   exult with trembling,
Accept correction
   lest he become angry and you perish along the way
   when his anger suddenly blazes up.
Blessed are all who take refuge in him!

This psalm is an early composition of pre-Israelite origin that was adapted to celebrate the accession, or the anniversary of the accession, of the Davidic king to the throne in Jerusalem. It presupposes the ritual of coronation that can be pieced together from other biblical texts (see, e.g., 1 Kgs 1:32-48). It may be divided as follows: (1) description of the vassal nations in revolt (vv. 1-3); (2) the Lord's response to this situation (vv. 4-6); (3) the Lord's oracle announcing the king's legitimacy and firm rule (vv. 7-9); (4) the Lord's admonition to the vassal kings (and indirectly to the Davidic king) to obey the divine will (vv. 10-11).

In the first section the psalmist describes the dangers of interregnum. In the transition from one Davidic king to another, vassal nations, that is, foreign nations subject to the Davidic king as overlord, invariably seize the opportunity to rebel and throw off the Davidic yoke. In the absence of a king balance and harmony are jeopardized. It is likely that a temple choir sings of this international plot in verses 1-2 while a special choir quotes their intent in verse 3: "Let us break their shackles / and cast off their chains from us!" In the second section the Lord's reaction echoes from heaven to earth. In verses 4-5 the temple choir proclaims that reaction whereby laughter gives way to anger. The message is that the Lord is very much in control. In verse 6 the Lord speaks through a prophet or court official who anoints the crown prince.

In the third section a prophet or court official also speaks on behalf of the Lord, citing the written document of legitimating, thereby proclaiming the king authentic. He is nothing less than the Lord's son (v. 7). Because of that status, the Lord empowers the new Davidic king to exercise world dominion and thus restore the world to harmony and balance (vv. 8-9). In the final section the vassal kings are urged to comply and do homage to the Lord lest they become victims of his anger (vv. 10-11). The message for them is obedience to the new Davidic king since the Lord rules the world through him.

For the people gathered at the coronation ceremony this psalm evoked the attitude of "Happy days are here again!" It was indeed an atmosphere of orientation since the Lord's pledged word guaranteed peace, security, and hope. Although the threat of vassal nations was a reality only for a limited period of time, it did serve to underline the Lord's commitment to the Davidic king and through him to the people. Thus, while this psalm is a prayer for the institution, it is also a prayer for those protected by the institution.

Israel never regarded the king as a god. However, in the development of the Davidic kingship with Solomon and the temple, the distance between the king and the people widened. This royal psalm implied more than "Hail to the Chief." It made the head of state the object of flattery and excessive praise. The idea of divine sonship, even though it was adoptive sonship, tended to blur the distinction that the covenant with Israel had established between the divine and the human.

At prayer we are confronted with the disharmony and disorder in our world and our own royal ego. Our temptation is to interpret our royal status as a condition that admits us to the world of the divine and thereby excludes us and indeed exempts us from the world of the ordinary, the profane. We note that we find it consoling to isolate ourselves in that divine world and neglect our royal charges. We are anesthetized into thinking that our coronation means a goal already achieved, not a goal to be achieved. We dare not think that "the one enthroned in heaven" (v. 4) will laugh at us. Yet we must conclude that such thinking and acting are a distortion of our royal condition. Only a royalty that unshackles itself from heaven (v. 3) and immerses itself in things of earth is genuine royalty. It is only when we create harmony and order among our subjects that we have truly earned the title of king or queen. Unfortunately the temptation faced by the Davidic king to blur the distinction between the sacred and the profane is healthy and very much alive in our midst.

## Psalm 110
## God Appoints the King both King and Priest

¹A psalm of David.
The LORD says to my lord:
    "Sit at my right hand,
    while I make your enemies your footstool."
²The scepter of your might:
    the LORD extends your strong scepter from Zion.
    Have dominion over your enemies!
³Yours is princely power from the day of your birth.
    In holy splendor before the daystar,
    like dew I begot you.
⁴The LORD has sworn and will not waver:
    "You are a priest forever in the manner of Melchizedek."
⁵At your right hand is the Lord,
    who crushes kings on the day of his wrath,
⁶Who judges nations, heaps up corpses,
    crushes heads across the wide earth,
⁷Who drinks from the brook by the wayside
    and thus holds high his head.

This psalm is both a very ancient and a very difficult one. (For an appreciation of its difficulty at the time of Jesus, see Matt 22:41-46; Mark 12:35-37; Luke 20:41-44.) Its setting is clearly the coronation of the new Davidic king. In terms of structure it seems to include three oracles recited by a court official. The first oracle (vv. 1-2) assures the king of victory over his enemies. The second oracle (v. 3) announces the adoptive sonship of the king. The third oracle (vv. 4-7) proclaims the king's future military victories as well as his status as priest.

In verse 1 the expression "my lord" refers to the Davidic king. By his position, namely, enthroned at God's right hand (v. 5), he enjoys a very close relationship with the Lord. The image of the enemies as a footstool captures the king's military domination. In the ancient Near East victorious kings put their feet on the prostrate bodies of their foes (see Josh 10:24). Verse 2 implies that Zion/Jerusalem is the center of the universe from which the king exercises his power and sovereignty. According to verse 3 the day of the coronation is regarded as the day of birth of the king as the Lord's adopted son (see Pss 2:7; 89:27-28). The "dew" may refer to the mysterious origin of this adoption (see Job 38:28). Possibly the "daystar" alludes to the time prior to creation (see Prov 8:22).

The third oracle begins with the Lord's solemn oath that the Davidic king is an eternal king like Melchizedek. Melchizedek was the ancient king of Salem/Jerusalem who also functioned as a priest in blessing Abram (see Gen 14:18-20). We know from some biblical texts that David and Solomon performed not only regal functions but also priestly ones (see 2 Sam 6:17-18; 24:25; 1 Kgs 8:5). In verses 5-7 the question is, who is the subject of these statements? Possibly the Lord is the subject only at the beginning of verse 5 (he is at the left of the king) and at the end of verse 7 (he holds high the head of the king). Elsewhere in this section the king enjoys worldwide dominion by crushing his enemies and governing them. The drink from the brook by the wayside may be an element in the rite of royal consecration (see 1 Kgs 1:33, 38).

At prayer this psalm may recall the effects of our baptism. Through baptism we become not only prophets and rulers but also priests. Baptism, therefore, empowers us to worship. By sharing in Eucharist, for example, we exercise our prerogative of priesthood. Rather than dwelling on the personal dimension of our status, we are urged to focus on its communal dimension. Hence in exercising our priestly role in worship, we must recall those to whom we minister. Our sisters and brothers have a right to the outcome of worship, namely, concern for and service to our God's family. Far from being a purely individualistic function, our baptism, our priesthood is by its very nature a call to action for others.

## Psalm 101
## Norm of Life for Rulers

[1]A psalm of David.

I

I sing of mercy and justice;
 to you, LORD, I sing praise.
[2]I study the the way of integrity;
 when will you come to me?
I act with integrity of heart
 within my household.
[3]I do not allow into my presence anything base.
 I hate wrongdoing;
 I will have no part of it.
[4]May the devious heart keep far from me;
 the wicked I will not acknowledge.
[5]Whoever slanders a neighbor in secret
 I will reduce to silence.
Haughty eyes and arrogant hearts
 I cannot endure.

II

[6]I look to the faithful of the land
 to sit at my side.
Whoever follows the way of integrity
 is the one to enter my service.
[7]No one who practices deceit
 can remain within my house.
No one who speaks falsely
 can last in my presence.
[8]Morning after morning I clear all the wicked from the land,
 to rid the city of the LORD of all doers of evil.

The setting for this psalm seems to be the coronation of the new Davidic king. It is likely that the psalm presents a dialogue between the king and a court official about the fitting conduct of the royal leader and his appropriate relationship with the people. The structure is as follows: (1) introduction (v. 1); (2) body (vv. 2-7): (a) general statement about the proper moral behavior of the king (vv. 2-3a), and (b) manner in which the king will carry out this ideal conduct (vv. 3b-7—vv. 3b-5 = negative formulation, vv. 6-7 = positive formulation); (3) conclusion sealing the king's promise (v. 8). The theme of the psalm is the peace and order among God's people that is made possible by the practice of justice.

In the introduction (v. 1) the poet sings of the Lord's covenant loyalty to the king and his people and of the king's justice whereby he provides for right order and peace. Verses 2-3a present the royal code of conduct: "the way of integrity," integrity of heart in the king's house, rejection of anything base in his presence.

In the negative formulation of this conduct (vv. 3b-5) the poet first mentions the king's attitude toward wrongdoing (v. 3b) and follows this up with a triple specification of wrongdoing: the devious of heart who will not be acknowledged (v. 4b), the slanderer who is to be silenced (v. 5a), and the one with haughty eyes and arrogant heart who is not to be endured (v. 5b). In the positive formulation of royal conduct (vv. 6-7) the psalmist develops the king's attitude toward the people. As companions he will seek only those faithful to God (v. 6a). Moreover, he will expect certain characteristics of such people: the way of integrity (v. 6b), avoiding deceit (v. 7a), and speaking the truth so as to qualify as an advisor to the king (v. 7b). Both the king and the people are to be distinguished by proper ethical living. The conclusion (v. 8) alludes to the role of the king as judge in the administration of justice that customarily took place in the morning (see 2 Sam 15:2-3; Jer 21:11-12).

The notion of harmony and well-being reflected in this psalm suggests the interaction of wisdom and appropriate royal conduct. The accent lies on the creation of a peaceful and wholesome community. Justice and politics are hardly opposites in establishing this climate. What disrupts this climate is the disharmony brought about by those who speak and act in such a way that the common good and total well-being are endangered. What is important in avoiding such disruption is the mutual effort of the king and the people. While the king is commissioned to provide justice and good order (see Prov 2:12; 4:14, 22), the people are also committed to covenant responsibility. To be in covenant means to provide for all, especially the weakest in the community.

At prayer we reflect on our oaths, promises, vows, and so forth. Simply by being members of society, we have obligations toward others. By belonging to a faith community, we have our theological grounding for those obligations, namely, covenant. Perhaps we will recall the inaugurations of our presidents when we anticipate the administration's platform. Hopefully we will also recollect our own enthusiastic responses on such occasions. "Ask not what your country can do for you; ask what you can do for your country" captures part of our response at least.

We must also include somewhat less grandiose inaugurations, for example, marriage vows, job commitments, or family promises. We have to examine our consciences and inquire whether or not we have been true to our royal code of conduct. At the same time we must ask whether or not we have supported and helped those who rule over us. Peace and harmony will emerge only at the cost of our own efforts.

### Psalm 72
### A Prayer for the King

¹Of Solomon.

I

²O God, give your judgment to the king;
    your justice to the king's son;
That he may govern your people with justice,
    your oppressed with right judgment,
³That the mountains may yield their bounty for the people,
    and the hills great abundance,
⁴That he may defend the oppressed among the people,
    save the children of the poor and crush the oppressor.

II

⁵May they fear you with the sun,
    and before the moon, through all generations.
⁶May he be like rain coming down upon the fields,
    like showers watering the earth,
⁷That abundance may flourish in his days,
    great bounty, till the moon be no more.

III

⁸May he rule from sea to sea,
    from the river to the ends of the earth.
⁹May his foes kneel before him,
    his enemies lick the dust.

¹⁰May the kings of Tarshish and the islands bring tribute,
  the kings of Sheba and Seba offer gifts.
¹¹May all kings bow before him,
  all nations serve him.
¹²For he rescues the poor when they cry out,
  the oppressed who have no one to help.
¹³He shows pity to the needy and the poor
  and saves the lives of the poor.
¹⁴From extortion and violence he redeems them,
  for precious is their blood in his sight.

IV

¹⁵Long may he live, receiving gold from Sheba,
  prayed for without cease, blessed day by day.
¹⁶May wheat abound in the land,
  flourish even on the mountain heights.
May his fruit be like that of Lebanon,
  and flourish in the city like the grasses of the land.
¹⁷May his name be forever;
  as long as the sun, may his name endure.
May the tribes of the earth give blessings with his name;
  may all the nations regard him as favored.
¹⁸Blessed be the LORD God, the God of Israel,
  who alone does wonderful deeds.
¹⁹Blessed be his glorious name forever;
  may he fill all the earth with his glory.
Amen and amen.

²⁰The end of the psalms of David, son of Jesse.

This psalm was recited on the occasion of the king's coronation and/or its anniversary. Borrowing from the court style of the ancient Near East, it stresses the motifs of justice, peace, long life, and worldwide rule. The basis of this hope is, of course, the Lord's promise to the Davidic dynasty. The psalm may be divided as follows: (1) introduction summarizing the Lord's promise (vv. 1-3); (2) a series of strophes praising the king and anticipating fulfillment of his royal duties (vv. 4-7, 8-11, 12-14, 15); (3) conclusion emphasizing fertility and justice that look back to the introduction (vv. 16-17). (Verses 18-20 are an addition, forming the conclusion of books 1 [Pss 1–41] and 2 [Pss 42–72] of the book of Psalms.)

In the introduction (vv. 1-3) the psalmist interprets the meaning of justice and judgment. These royal qualities whereby right order and truth prevail are meant to result in the good of the people. Hence in verse 2 the poet observes that the people and the oppressed in particular are to benefit from these qualities. In verse 3 the poet invokes the blessings of fertility on the people. The word "bounty" translates the Hebrew word *shalom* meaning "peace." However, *shalom* is more than the cessation of hostilities between warring factions. It is the most complete integration of life's blessings (physical, emotional, etc.) throughout Israel and the world at large. It is the fullest union of heaven and earth, the Lord and humans.

In the central section (vv. 4-15) the psalmist prays that the king bestow fertility on the people (v. 6: "like rain . . . like showers") that will result in abundance and great bounty (v. 7). In verses 8-11 the psalmist focuses on the power and expansion of the Davidic dynasty. In its florid court language that kingdom is to extend from the borders of Egypt to the Euphrates River and from Transjordan to the islands of the Mediterranean Sea (v. 8). Tribute (v. 10) is to be forthcoming from the far west (Tarshish and the islands) and from the south (Sheba and Seba) while due homage comes from the rulers of the world, whether friend (v. 11) or foe (v. 9). However, in the midst of such power the psalmist does not neglect the prime objects of royal concern: the poor, the oppressed, the needy (vv. 12-13). The combination of "redeem" and "blood" (v. 14) suggests that the king is bound to act on behalf of those suffering because of a certain kinship bond (see Lev 25:23-55).

In the conclusion the psalmist seems to allude to Genesis 12:3, where Abram (through the Davidic kings) is to be a source of blessing for all the tribes and nations of the earth (v. 17). Against this background of the Davidic line the king's name and fame will endure (v. 17) on the condition that the king has met the needs of his people. It is only that condition that will ensure fertility and well-being (v. 16).

At prayer we must move beyond the record of the Davidic kings. By and large, they were dismal failures—they provided for themselves, not the people. Nonetheless the focus of the psalm is the king as person for others. Specifically the psalmist underlines the virtue of humility. By this virtue the king realizes all too vividly that he can fulfill his obligations only by dependence on God. Like the ordinary Israelite, the king too must invoke God's assistance so that he can deal with his weaknesses.

At prayer, as we attempt to create harmony and prosperity for our royal charges, we must frankly admit that we cannot attain that goal merely by our own efforts. Prayer is not the application of an unflinching, iron will that hopefully results in accomplishments. Prayer is the awareness that to fulfill our office we need to lean upon Another and thus gather strength by noting our weaknesses. At prayer we come to realize that we can be kings and queens for our royal subjects only by being loyal subjects of the Great King. After the manner of this psalm, our vision must also be universal. It must embrace all (v. 17).

## Psalm 45
## Song for a Royal Wedding

¹For the leader; according to "Lilies." A *maskil* of the Korahites.
A love song.
I
²My heart is stirred by a noble theme,
    as I sing my ode to the king.
    My tongue is the pen of a nimble scribe.
II
³You are the most handsome of men;
    fair speech has graced your lips,
    for God has blessed you forever.
⁴Gird your sword upon your hip, mighty warrior!
    In splendor and majesty ride on triumphant!
⁵In the cause of truth, meekness, and justice
    may your right hand show your wondrous deeds.
⁶Your arrows are sharp;
    peoples will cower at your feet;
    the king's enemies will lose heart.
⁷Your throne, O God, stands forever;
    your royal scepter is a scepter for justice.
⁸You love justice and hate wrongdoing;
    therefore God, your God, has anointed you
    with the oil of gladness above your fellow kings.
⁹With myrrh, aloes, and cassia
    your robes are fragrant.

From ivory-paneled palaces
    stringed instruments bring you joy.
¹⁰Daughters of kings are your lovely wives;
    a princess arrayed in Ophir's gold
    comes to stand at your right hand.

III

¹¹Listen, my daughter, and understand;
    pay me careful heed.
Forget your people and your father's house,
    ¹²that the king might desire your beauty.
He is your lord;
    ¹³honor him, daughter of Tyre.
Then the richest of the people
    will seek your favor with gifts.
¹⁴All glorious is the king's daughter as she enters,
    her raiment threaded with gold;
¹⁵In embroidered apparel she is led to the king.
    The maids of her train are presented to the king.
¹⁶They are led in with glad and joyous acclaim;
    they enter the palace of the king.

IV

¹⁷The throne of your fathers your sons will have;
    you shall make them princes through all the land.
¹⁸I will make your name renowned through all generations;
    thus nations shall praise you forever.

This royal psalm is the celebration of a royal wedding. ("Lilies" in v. 1 refers to the tune, or musical setting, to which the psalm should be sung.) Although its original setting was perhaps the marriage of a northern king of Israel (see "Tyre" in v. 13), it was eventually adapted to the southern kingdom of Judah and its Davidic dynasty. (This may explain why the king is addressed as "God" in verse 7, that is, a sacred person beyond the ordinary—see Isa 7:14.) The psalm may be divided as follows: (1) introduction by the court poet (v. 2); (2) the poet's praise of the king (vv. 3-10); (3) address by the queen mother to the princess chosen (vv. 11-13); (4) a description of the bride's apparel and the procession (vv. 14-16); (5) the poet's concluding address to the king (vv. 17-18).

A possible scenario for this psalm is the following. An eloquent and handsome king, who is a victor in battle and a just ruler, is going to celebrate a marriage. There are various pretenders of royal blood and he has fallen in love with one of them. His mother, that is, the queen mother mentioned in verse 10 (read "queen" instead of "princess"), assists him in the ceremony by soliciting the consent of the one chosen (vv. 11-12). The other pretenders now withdraw and the lucky princess is led to the king (v. 15a) while her entourage is led to the palace (v. 16). Finally the poet wishes the king sons upon whom he will confer offices (v. 17).

The personages in the poem are, therefore, the king, the queen mother, the various royal princesses (would-be wives of the king), and the princess selected by the king along with her entourage. However, the central figure is clearly the king. The court poet sings his praises in verses 3-10. The queen mother observes in verse 13 that because of the king's choice, the lucky princess will enjoy the attention of the wealthy. Finally in verse 17 the poet implies that the successor to the throne will be the son of this fortunate woman.

While the climate of the psalm is clearly festive because of the marriage of the handsome king and the beautiful princess, the psalmist also emphasizes other values. According to verse 5 the king champions truth and justice. According to verse 8 he advocates the right order of society (the promotion of justice and the overthrow of wickedness). Thus the king adds to his beauty a sense of covenant loyalty and fidelity. The lucky lady is getting a first-class husband!

At prayer we reflect on the exuberance of marriage celebrations but more particularly on the sense of loyalty and fidelity demanded by such celebrations. As kings and queens, human spouses are to create an atmosphere of stability and equilibrium in their relationships. As this psalm suggests, qualities such as truth and justice contribute to this atmosphere.

At prayer we cannot exclude the analogy of royal marriages from the relationship of a bishop to his diocese, especially the Bishop of Rome. Here too the covenant qualities mentioned in this psalm come to the fore. True harmony means that the people are served, not the bishop, that the common good is fostered, not personal ambition, that the obligations of the bishop are stressed, not his rights. At the same time we must honestly ask ourselves how we have assisted the bishop

and other church leaders in promoting the well-being of our local diocese or faith community. Royalty makes such demands. At prayer we
dare not avoid all the implications of such marriages. The demands of
such royal marriages are anything but light.

## Psalm 20
### Prayer for the King in Time of War

¹For the leader. A psalm of David.

I

²The Lord answer you in time of distress;
    the name of the God of Jacob defend you!
³May he send you help from the sanctuary,
    from Zion be your support.
⁴May he remember your every offering,
    graciously accept your burnt offering,

*Selah*

⁵Grant what is in your heart,
    fulfill your every plan.
⁶May we shout for joy at your victory,
    raise the banners in the name of our God.
    The Lord grant your every petition!

II

⁷Now I know the Lord gives victory
    to his anointed.
He will answer him from the holy heavens
    with a strong arm that brings victory.
⁸Some rely on chariots, others on horses,
    but we on the name of the Lord our God.
⁹They collapse and fall,
    but we stand strong and firm.
¹⁰Lord, grant victory to the king;
    answer when we call upon you.

The setting for this psalm is a time of warfare. The king and the people
gather in the temple and offer a prayer for the success of the king's
military venture. According to the promise to the Davidic dynasty, a
threat to the king and his people is a threat to the Lord (see 2 Sam

7:16). Hence the Lord must intervene. The psalm may be divided as follows: (1) petition by the people before the king goes into battle (vv. 2-6); (2) prayer of confidence by the people that God will give a positive answer to their petition (vv. 7-10). Between the two parts there may have been a solemn oracle by a priest assuring both the king and the people of victory (see Ps 12:6).

In the first section the name of God is significant (v. 2). Far from being a mere designation, a name conjures up the person. To a certain extent it is the name of God, which is that all-powerful agent that will provide help (see Ps 44:6). By the same token God's remembering (v. 4) is not an abstract recollection. Rather, it is God's readiness to act on behalf of his people (see Gen 8:1; Exod 2:24). The burnt offering (v. 4) is a whole burnt offering. This is probably part of a prewar ritual wherein Israel invoked God's help (see 1 Sam 7:7-11). The banners (v. 6) may refer to the insignia proper to each tribe (see Num 1:52; 2:2) or the practice of keeping important trophies in the temple (see Num 21:8-9; 2 Kgs 18:4).

In the second section the psalmist emphasizes the basis of the people's confidence. It is God's strength (v. 7: "strong arm") that is linked to his name (v. 8) that will win the day. Military armaments by themselves (v. 8) are not decisive (see Isa 31:1). The author captures the contrast very well in verse 9: while those who depend on chariots and horses "collapse and fall," those who rely on the Lord "stand strong and firm." It is worth noting that the final verse (v. 10) reechoes the opening verse.

At prayer this psalm provides a number of options. Faced with injustice, we are urged to take immediate action and redress the wrongs suffered by the oppressed. If the situation does not call for instantaneous response, we are counseled to wait and to trust. Without neglecting our human resources, we are asked to make room for God's power to turn things around. The setting of this psalm in the community gathered together in the temple may prompt us to seek advice and help from the members of our community. Ultimately only an atmosphere of prayer will enable us to make the right decision. As Ecclesiastes puts it, "There is an appointed time for everything, / and a time for every affair under the heavens" (3:1). As experience shows, the rush to arms is too often a disastrous option.

## New Testament

### Mark 1:14-15; 8:27-33

[14]After John had been arrested, Jesus came to Galilee proclaiming the gospel of God: [15]"This is the time of fulfillment. The kingdom of God is at hand. Repent, and believe in the gospel."

[27]Now Jesus and his disciples set out for the villages of Caesarea Philippi. Along the way he asked his disciples, "Who do people say that I am?" [28]They said in reply, "John the Baptist, others Elijah, still others one of the prophets." [29]And he asked them, "But who do you say that I am?" Peter said to him in reply, "You are the Messiah." [30]Then he warned them not to tell anyone about him.

[31]He began to teach them that the Son of Man must suffer greatly and be rejected by the elders, the chief priests, and the scribes, and be killed, and rise after three days. [32]He spoke this openly. Then Peter took him aside and began to rebuke him. [33]At this he turned around and, looking at his disciples, rebuked Peter and said, "Get behind me, Satan. You are thinking not as God does, but as human beings do."

In Mark 1:14 Jesus announced that God's kingdom had finally arrived. By using the term "kingdom," Jesus proclaimed that God's plan of providing for all the people had now begun in his person. "Kingdom" referred to the ideal of leadership expressed in the royal psalms. It conjured up all the expectations that the king would rule over his state in such a way that justice and peace would be the hallmark of his reign. "Kingdom" connoted power but power channeled toward the common good, not personal advantage. In particular, "kingdom" meant that the poor, the needy, the down and out would be conspicuous objects of the king's concern. Jesus' message, therefore, was nothing short of good news. God was taking a final and definitive hand in human history and Jesus was to be the catalyst in that unique event.

In carrying out his Father's plan for the kingdom, Jesus communicated a profound sense of basic human values. He preached that to find oneself one should lose oneself (Mark 8:34-35), that to be first one must become a servant (Mark 9:33-35), that to be great one must be small (Mark 10:42-44). The radical message of the kingdom was that exercising the office of leader meant forgetting oneself in ongoing service to those being led. The royal theology of the ancient Near East and particularly of the Davidic dynasty took flesh, not only in the words of Jesus, but also in his actions and hence his way of life. The message of the kingdom was simply a code of conduct for all would-be kings and queens.

Jesus had misgivings about the popular notions of kingship, that is, messiahship, that focused primarily on the power and prestige of the ruler. Realizing the corrupting tendencies of power and prestige, he resolved to win the hearts of his hearers, not merely buy them off. At Caesarea Philippi Mark presents Jesus as acknowledging the title of Messiah given to him by Peter. However, Mark goes on to show Jesus qualifying the notion of Messiah. Jesus would attain his messiahship only as a result of passion, death, and resurrection. This Messiah is a suffering Messiah.

As Mark continues, this interpretation of royal power is something that Peter regards as totally contradictory. For Peter, power and suffering do not go hand in hand. However, Mark concludes the episode by having Jesus observe that Peter's position is a perversion of God's plan. To accept Peter's view is to align oneself with the self-seeking and dehumanizing party of Satan. In the final analysis Peter is receiving a lecture on the proper understanding of the royal psalms.

In his speeches in the Acts of the Apostles, Luke uses the royal psalms to interpret Jesus' exaltation. In Acts 2:30 he cites Psalm 132:11, which says that one of David's descendants would sit upon his throne. In Acts 2:34-35 he quotes Psalm 110:1 to show that through his resurrection Jesus has been enthroned in his glory as Lord. In Acts 13:33 he uses Psalm 2:7, claiming that Jesus is properly called "son" on the day of the resurrection and hence shares universal kingship with God. For Luke, therefore, it is through the psalms that the feelings and attitudes of Jesus in accomplishing his mission are powerfully expressed.

## Summary of the theology of the royal psalms

1. These psalms must lead us to focus on both the institution and ourselves, especially in considering virtues and vices.
2. They are calculated to address us as empowered people who must reach out to sustain and protect our royal charges.

3. They are to remind us of our need for humility so that we may draw strength from our God in exercising our office.

4. They also teach us not to abdicate and give up on the proper discharge of our duties. Offices are always for others; hence our God chooses to need us for others.

5. The praying of the royal psalms long after the collapse of the Davidic dynasty teaches us that the sinful institution is always linked to the Sinless One.

# CHAPTER 6

# Out of the Pits

## The Laments

### Orientation versus disorientation

The psalms of descriptive praise, the psalms of trust or confidence, the wisdom psalms, and the royal psalms (at least those studied in the last chapter) imply a world of logic and cohesiveness. They speak to the times when order and tranquillity are in command, when logic and reason hold sway, when balance and equilibrium rule. But our human experience must candidly confess those times when chaos and disorder take over, when turbulence and panic assume control, when pain and frustration manage our lives. Our world may be in the process of falling or may have already fallen apart. We suffer the death of a loved one. We contract a serious illness. We become the object of slander or gossip. We find it increasingly difficult to pay the rent or the mortgage. Our former friends reject us. How difficult it now becomes to pray, "The LORD is my shepherd; / there is nothing I lack" (Ps 23:1).

All too painfully our human vulnerability betrays itself. When tragedy strikes, we discover our pitiful weakness. We have to acknowledge that we are subject to interest rates, the caprices of human friendship, and the destructibility of the human body. Our world is collapsing and with typically human know-how we seek to rebuild it the old-fashioned way. Indeed these efforts at reconstruction are the greatest source of disillusion. We invoke the tried-and-true remedies of the past but they do not work. We recite the doctrines of our church community but they are ineffective. We remember that the God who afflicts us is the God who loves us (see Job 5:17-18) but it is not enough. We cling to the ever new miracles of modern medicine but they do not do the job. Basically we do not want the securities of the past to disappear; we are unwilling to let go.

Loneliness is the specter that haunts us. We feel we are individuals cut off from the mainstream of life and condemned to a hell where the gnawing pain is isolation. Community no longer exists; the only reality is aloofness and disinterest on the part of others. It is now that we admit that distress and lack of community go hand in hand. We angrily concede that the source of our frustration is the inability to communicate. Yet at the same time we begin to glimpse the reality of redemption, that is, pain that is not communicated is pain that cannot be healed.

At prayer we deal with the real experiences of life. In the presence of our God we put aside all pretense and make-believe. We know that our frustration is real and that an iron-willed effort to forget it will only increase the frustration. In communing with our God we are exhorted to face life with all its agony. We are challenged not to resort to never-never land where pain is not real and anguish not genuine. In honest dialogue with our God the fact is that the bottom is falling out of life. However, those less-than-beautiful moments are now the new raw material for prayer.

## Laments

In both individual and communal laments, which express a state of disorientation, we have to deal with a Person. In these prayers there is One to whom both the individual and the community can and must turn in order to be healed. Hence we talk *to* our God; we do not talk *about* him. The laments do not simply register the data about our distressing situation. They are not a digital readout enumerating all our ills. The prayer of lament is not a gripe session. The Lord is a person, not a machine. As Claus Westermann has emphasized, the laments move on to petition and finally to praise. They are protestations rooted in the power of our God to intervene. They also contain an atmosphere of expectation that our God will hear and act on our behalf.

The laments are a powerful demonstration of the centrality of covenant. Because of the triangular nature of covenant (the Lord, the community, and the individual), the Lord has a claim on us both as individuals and members of the community. However, we also have a claim on the Lord, both as individuals and members of the community. This covenant reality helps to explain the element of boldness that is so characteristic of these psalms (see Pss 44:24; 88:14-15). Because of the nature of covenant, we have the right to address this God and ask for a hearing.

The Lord thus becomes the God of my/our problem. What the laments really presuppose is that my/our problem necessarily becomes God's problem. Far from being unconcerned, the Lord continues to have a vested interest in us and thus remains a committed covenant partner. That there is a God of my/our problem means the death of solitude and isolation. We are linked to Another.

The Lord's problem also becomes my/our problem. The other dimension of covenant is that the Lord's problem, namely, other people, necessarily becomes my and/or the community's problem. When others are in disorientation, our God is in disorientation and hence appeals to us. The covenant nature of our relationship is the ground for the involvement of the individual and/or community in the needs and frustrations of others. The laments thus continue to be an eloquent appeal to "get involved." We cannot pray to this God merely one-on-one. To know the Lord in prayer is also to be aware of the Lord's extended family and their needs.

The laments admit different degrees of acceptance or denial. They speak of people who are just beginning to break free of their dependence on the old securities as well as of those who have accepted their problem as the springboard for reorientation. (Psalm 88 is the only lament that does not get beyond disorientation.) Hence these prayers do not refer to only one level in the process of disorientation. The laments are as large as life and reflect a spectrum moving from the tenacious grip of the old to the loving acceptance of the new.

Both the individual and the communal laments show the following basic structure: (1) address with an introductory cry for help; (2) lament; (3) confession of trust or confidence of being heard; (4) petition; (5) vow of praise. A considerable problem is the explanation of the transition from distress to relief. A common view is that a temple official pronounces an oracle of salvation that resolves the problem of the petitioner. Despite difficulties with this view, what is clear is the transformation of the person or persons. Without doubt change does occur—*shalom* does return.

## Psalm 3
### Threatened but Trusting

¹A psalm of David, when he fled from his son Absalom.

I

²How many are my foes, LORD!
    How many rise against me!
³How many say of me,
    "There is no salvation for him in God."

                                                            *Selah*

⁴But you, LORD, are a shield around me;
    my glory, you keep my head high.

II

⁵With my own voice I will call out to the LORD,
    and he will answer me from his holy mountain.

                                                            *Selah*

⁶I lie down and I fall asleep,
    [and] I will wake up, for the LORD sustains me.
⁷I do not fear, then, thousands of people
    arrayed against me on every side.

III

⁸Arise, LORD! Save me, my God!
    For you strike the cheekbone of all my foes;
    you break the teeth of the wicked.
⁹Salvation is from the LORD!
    May your blessing be upon your people!

                                                            *Selah*

This psalm may be divided as follows: (1) appeal and lament (vv. 2-3); (2) trust (vv. 4-7); (3) petition (v. 8); (4) vow of praise (v. 9). There are three characters in the psalm: the Lord, the psalmist, and the foes. The psalmist sees himself surrounded by a multitude of soldiers who are ready to attack him (v. 2). It is their contention that God is incapable of saving him (v. 3). However, the Lord as the Divine Warrior stands between the psalmist and the vast enemy force. (The "Divine Warrior" is an early Israelite understanding of the Lord as the commander-in-chief who fights Israel's wars and brings them victory—see, e.g., Josh 6:1-27.) The image of a shield (v. 4) captures the Lord's military presence. The psalmist continues this expression of faith by observing in verse 5 that the Lord will answer him from his holy mountain when he cries out. This expression is the precise opposite of the enemies' contention in verse 3 that the Lord will not intervene to save the psalmist.

The Lord intervenes dramatically. It is fitting that the psalmist reserves this action for the end of the poem: the Lord shatters the cheekbone and breaks the teeth of all his foes (v. 8). However, prior to describing this action, the psalmist is careful to underline the attitude of trust. Thus, when the enemies rise to attack him (v. 2), the psalmist lies down and sleeps (v. 6), so that the Lord can arise (v. 8) for the victory. Even in its most dangerous moments life continues to function according to its basic rhythm. Sleep, therefore, symbolizes here the assurance of victory. The psalmist is certain that, when morning comes, the Divine Warrior will begin the combat whose inevitable outcome is the defeat of the foes.

In this poem the psalmist clearly experiences disorientation. In the face of a huge and menacing army the harmony of life has disintegrated. However, the crisis (the military symbol is flexible enough to cover a variety of human predicaments) becomes a faith opportunity. The description of confidence that culminates in sleep suggests that the psalmist has been willing to let go and accept the intervention of his God. Hence disorientation will not be the last word. The darkness is not insuperable. The day is dawning, the moment when the Divine Warrior will definitively intervene.

At prayer we cannot dismiss the shocks in our lives. Indeed they are so real that they appear to impinge on the harmony of our prayer. However, this appearance is deceiving because such shocks rightly become the raw material of prayer. To find healing, we must turn to Another who does not regard our woes as trivial but as the stuff out of which we can grow. Without dismissing human effort, this psalm emphasizes the fact that we cannot resolve all problems by ourselves. We must learn to lean upon Another and see that dependence, not as the loss of autonomy, but as the growth of our relationship.

In the other direction, this psalm challenges us to be the Divine Warrior for others. The implication of this title, namely, concern for one's people at critical moments, is imposed on us by reason of covenant. At prayer we must not cease to picture our God as beset by worries and afflicted with pain. Our God's worries and afflictions (other people) become ours. The disturbing question is, will at least some of God's people sleep tonight because we have committed ourselves to action in the morning? In effect, we have to offset the contention of the foes that God will not save the psalmist (v. 3).

## Psalm 22
### The Prayer of an Innocent Person

[1]For the leader; according to "The deer of the dawn." A psalm of David.

I

[2]My God, my God, why have you abandoned me?
  Why so far from my call for help,
    from my cries of anguish?
[3]My God, I call by day, but you do not answer;
  by night, but I have no relief.
[4]Yet you are enthroned as the Holy One;
  you are the glory of Israel.
[5]In you our fathers trusted;
  they trusted and you rescued them.
[6]To you they cried out and they escaped;
  in you they trusted and were not disappointed.
[7]But I am a worm, not a man,
  scorned by men, despised by the people.
[8]All who see me mock me;
  they curl their lips and jeer;
  they shake their heads at me:
[9]"He relied on the LORD—let him deliver him;
  if he loves him, let him rescue him."
[10]For you drew me forth from the womb,
  made me safe at my mother's breasts.
[11]Upon you I was thrust from the womb;
  since my mother bore me you are my God.

¹²Do not stay far from me,
for trouble is near,
and there is no one to help.

II

¹³Many bulls surround me;
fierce bulls of Bashan encircle me.
¹⁴They open their mouths against me,
lions that rend and roar.
¹⁵Like water my life drains away;
all my bones are disjointed.
My heart has become like wax,
it melts away within me.
¹⁶As dry as a potsherd is my throat;
my tongue cleaves to my palate;
you lay me in the dust of death.
¹⁷Dogs surround me;
a pack of evildoers closes in on me.
They have pierced my hands and my feet;
¹⁸I can count all my bones.
They stare at me and gloat;
¹⁹they divide my garments among them;
for my clothing they cast lots.
²⁰But you, LORD, do not stay far off;
my strength, come quickly to help me.
²¹Deliver my soul from the sword,
my life from the grip of the dog.
²²Save me from the lion's mouth,
my poor life from the horns of wild bulls.

III

²³Then I will proclaim your name to my brethren;
in the assembly I will praise you:
²⁴"You who fear the LORD, give praise!
All descendants of Jacob, give honor;
show reverence, all descendants of Israel!
²⁵For he has not spurned or disdained
the misery of this poor wretch,
Did not turn away from me,
but heard me when I cried out.

²⁶I will offer praise in the great assembly;
    my vows I will fulfill before those who fear him.
²⁷The poor will eat their fill;
    those who seek the LORD will offer praise.
    May your hearts enjoy life forever!"
IV
²⁸All the ends of the earth
    will remember and turn to the LORD;
All the families of nations
    will bow low before him.
²⁹For kingship belongs to the LORD,
    the ruler over the nations.
³⁰All who sleep in the earth
    will bow low before God;
All who have gone down into the dust
    will kneel in homage.
³¹And I will live for the LORD;
    my descendants will serve you.
³²The generation to come will be told of the Lord,
    that they may proclaim to a people yet unborn
    the deliverance you have brought.

The original psalm consists of verses 2-22 (lament) and verses 23-27 (thanksgiving). The lament may be divided as follows: (1) invocation and cry for help (vv. 2-3); (2) motivation (vv. 4-6); (3) lament (vv. 7-9); (4) expression of confidence (vv. 10-11); (5) prayer for help (v. 12); (6) lament (vv. 13-19); (7) prayer for help (vv. 20-22). In verses 23-27 the psalmist celebrates a thanksgiving liturgy. He fulfills his vows (v. 26). In keeping with the theme of the lament proper there is a profession that the Lord has indeed heard (v. 25). Verses 28-32 are an expansion of the original thanksgiving. At a later date another member of God's community extended the poem to include the Gentiles (vv. 28-29), the sick and perhaps the dead (vv. 30-31), and the unborn (v. 32).

In verses 2-22 the psalmist is utterly innocent. He does not recite any previous sins. He does not inveigh against his enemies. Nonetheless he suffers. That suffering is depicted in symbols borrowed from the animal world: worm (v. 7), bulls (v. 14), dogs (vv. 17, 21), lion and wild bulls (v. 22). It also finds expression in images describing his bodily condition: soft bones (v. 15), heart like wax (v. 15), throat as dry as a potsherd (v. 16), tongue sticking to the palate (v. 16). The attitude of the people is hardly reassuring. They ridicule the psalmist since his condition gives evidence of sin (vv. 7-9). They stare and gloat (v. 18), anticipating the moment of death.

Interspersed are the protestations of confidence. Particularly noteworthy is the record of the Lord's previous interventions. Earlier generations were in straits yet God did not abandon them. Rather, they were delivered and saved (vv. 5-6). However, the pain mounts in the face of silence. As the Lord is seated on his throne in the sanctuary ready to accede to the needs of his people (v. 4), the only sound is deafening silence. This God appears to be deaf! However, by the time the psalmist reaches verse 23 there is a definite change. There is a movement from the seemingly unbending and deaf God to the Lord who is now "all ears."

At prayer we must ponder the price of commitment that is so often the source of disorientation. According to verse 9 the psalmist's life is bound up with his God—something that should result in reorientation according to the poet's scoffers. Instead of the quick and decisive movement to reorientation that we crave (v. 23), we may often hear the penetrating sound of silence. Because of this impasse, we naturally pose the question, is it reasonable to continue to trust? We are tempted to think that the Faithful One is more responsive to infidelity than fidelity. Yet in the face of inexplicable forces we are encouraged to cling to our God. Our life must still be grounded in the Lord as partner. This God is still *my* God (vv. 2-3). "For *you* drew me forth from the womb . . . Upon *you* I was thrust from the womb" (vv. 10-11; emphasis added).

At prayer we are perhaps challenged to assume the place of the deaf God. To those who do not hear encouragement and hope from their God we are asked to be present and listen. So often our task is not to offer rational explanations of seemingly irrational divine actions but to provide the ministry of listening and the ministry of presence. Whenever one human listens to another distraught human, the enthroned Holy One (v. 4) is present. Prayer thus becomes the occasion for bending God's ear in another direction.

## Psalm 39
## The Vanity of Life

¹For the leader, for Jeduthun. A psalm of David.

I

²I said, "I will watch my ways,
    lest I sin with my tongue;
    I will keep a muzzle on my mouth."
³Mute and silent before the wicked,
    I refrain from good things.
But my sorrow increases;
    ⁴my heart smolders within me.
In my sighing a fire blazes up,
    and I break into speech:

II

⁵LORD, let me know my end, the number of my days,
    that I may learn how frail I am.
⁶To be sure, you establish the expanse of my days;
    indeed, my life is as nothing before you.
    Every man is but a breath.

                                                        *Selah*

III

⁷Man goes about as a mere phantom;
    they hurry about, although in vain;
    he heaps up stores without knowing for whom.
⁸And now, LORD, for what do I wait?
    You are my only hope.
⁹From all my sins deliver me;
    let me not be the taunt of fools.
¹⁰I am silent and do not open my mouth
    because you are the one who did this.
¹¹Take your plague away from me;
    I am ravaged by the touch of your hand.
¹²You chastise man with rebukes for sin;
    like a moth you consume his treasures.
    Every man is but a breath.

                                                        *Selah*

¹³Listen to my prayer, LORD, hear my cry;
  do not be deaf to my weeping!
For I am with you like a foreigner,
  a refugee, like my ancestors.
¹⁴Turn your gaze from me, that I may smile
  before I depart to be no more.

This psalm is ultimately a study of the theology of security, a meditation on the irony of human existence in relation to the Existing One.
In light of the fleeting nature of life the basis of human confidence is
not a thing, a principle, a system. It is a person, namely, the Lord. The
poem may be divided as follows: (1) an introduction that hammers
home the conviction that silence is simply inadequate (vv. 2-4); (2) the
impermanence of human existence (vv. 5-8); (3) petition for deliverance
(vv. 9-12); (4) supplication for the hearing of the petition (vv. 13-14).

The psalmist was apparently the object of ridicule and verbal abuse
because of his religious convictions. Hence he resolved to curb his
mouth (vv. 2-3) rather than lash out against his opponents. However,
the resolution did not work. The psalmist's condition became all the
graver as he vainly attempted to refrain from speaking out (vv. 4-5).
The silence was hardly golden!

Instead of asking for the overthrow of his assailants, the poet now
proceeds to reflect on the human condition, in the tradition of Israel's
wisdom writers. After requesting knowledge of his own fleeting life (v.
4), the psalmist muses on the meaning of human life as such, not merely
his personal afflictions. All humans are but a breath (v. 6). The Hebrew
word translated as "breath" seems to mean irony, indicating a perception of the distance between pretense (what should be) and reality (what
actually is). In the style of Ecclesiastes (6:2, 12) he must conclude that
"he heaps up stores without knowing for whom" (v. 7). The plight of
the psalmist is now ironically linked to human existence in general.

In verses 9-12 the psalmist asks for deliverance. He seeks divine
help in a situation where humans are but a breath (v. 12). Despite the
vicious circle of human existence, he finds hope in the person of the
Lord. The psalmist has only two options: (1) to turn from what has
made human life the way it is or (2) to turn to God and accept. Electing
the second alternative, he surrenders to the Lord who, while aware of
his faults, is also capable of showing mercy. The psalmist does not ask

God to bring back his earlier thoughtless life. Rather, he now acknowledges God for having made human existence the way it is.

In his supplication (vv. 13-14) the psalmist seeks deliverance from his present predicament (vv. 13a, 14a). However, the motive for the Lord's intervention is the human condition itself. A foreigner (v. 13b) implies the notion of an outsider while refugee (v. 13b) connotes a displaced person. Such was the condition of Israel's ancestors, the patriarchs: they dwelt in the land but did not possess it. While the continuation of one's family on the land is a form of immortality, the psalmist concludes that the reality of the human condition is the security of dependence on the Lord, not the security of owning land. While this is not an afterlife in the traditional sense, it does contain the seed of the afterlife, namely, rootedness in the covenant God.

At prayer we cannot avoid the question of values, which is often at the bottom of our disorientation. What makes life congruous or incongruous? What overcomes the irony we experience? We must truly ask whether or not we merely count up our merits and so reduce our God to the level of the Heavenly Administrator. At prayer we must seek to encounter a God who is not the fiction of our virtuous deeds but the bedrock of our daily existence. As we seek to address our disorientation, we must make the strategic move from things to a person: "And now, LORD, for what do I wait? / *You* are my only hope" (v. 8; emphasis added).

Similarly we must offer deeply personal hope to the distraught of our world. Because of covenant, we are to be the sources of confidence, weak and fickle though we sometimes are! To those who find human existence drab and meaningless, we are to offer a new vision of life rooted in the Living One. Prayer is our source of energy for making hope the possession of others, so that foreigners and refugees may become full-fledged citizens. As members of God's family, we must reach out to all our relatives.

## Psalms 42–43
## Longing for God's Presence in the Temple

[1]For the leader. A *maskil* of the Korahites.

I

[2]As the deer longs for streams of water,
so my soul longs for you, O God.

³My soul thirsts for God, the living God.
     When can I enter and see the face of God?
⁴My tears have been my bread day and night,
     as they ask me every day, "Where is your God?"
⁵Those times I recall
     as I pour out my soul,
When I would cross over to the shrine of the Mighty One,
     to the house of God,
Amid loud cries of thanksgiving,
     with the multitude keeping festival.
⁶Why are you downcast, my soul;
     why do you groan within me?
Wait for God, for I shall again praise him,
     my savior and my God.
     II
⁷My soul is downcast within me;
     therefore I remember you
From the land of the Jordan and Hermon,
     from Mount Mizar,
⁸Deep calls to deep
     in the roar of your torrents,
And all your waves and breakers
     sweep over me.
⁹By day may the LORD send his mercy,
     and by night may his righteousness be with me!
     I will pray to the God of my life,
¹⁰I will say to God, my rock:
     "Why do you forget me?
Why must I go about mourning
     with the enemy oppressing me?"
¹¹It shatters my bones, when my adversaries reproach me,
     when they say to me every day: "Where is your God?"
¹²Why are you downcast, my soul,
     why do you groan within me?
Wait for God, for I shall again praise him,
     my savior and my God.
¹Grant me justice, O God;
     defend me from a faithless people;
     from the deceitful and unjust rescue me.

²You, O God, are my strength.
  Why then do you spurn me?
Why must I go about mourning,
  with the enemy oppressing me?
³Send your light and your fidelity,
  that they may be my guide;
Let them bring me to your holy mountain,
  to the place of your dwelling,
⁴That I may come to the altar of God,
  to God, my joy, my delight.
Then I will praise you with the harp,
  O God, my God.
⁵Why are you downcast, my soul?
  Why do you groan within me?
Wait for God, for I shall again praise him,
  my savior and my God.

These two psalms were originally a single poem. An indication of this is that the same refrain concludes each of the three strophes (42:1-6; 42:7-12; 43:1-5): "Why are you downcast, my soul? / Why do you groan within me? / Wait for God, for I shall again praise him, / my savior and my God" (43:5). There are two major images in the psalm: (1) water as life (42:1-6) and (2) water as death (42:7-12).

The psalmist is the object of ridicule because of his reliance on the Lord (42:4, 11). He suffers from the absence of God, although the precise cause (sickness, persecution, etc.) is not pinpointed. He finds himself in a mountainous area south of Mount Hermon (42:7), where he sees a deer desperately searching for water (42:2a). The psalmist then projects his experience onto the deer's (42:2b-3). The poet's whole being is now devoured by an animal thirst for God. In this same area close by the sources of the Jordan (42:7) he also experiences the thundering torrents that remind him of the destructive sea that God overcame in creation (Gen 1:2). Here the water is not life-giving—it is death-dealing (42:8). The psalmist resolves the tension of these aspects of the water by introducing the minor images of light and fidelity in 43:3.

The transition from disorientation to reorientation takes place in an inner dialogue. On one level of consciousness nostalgia and dismay predominate as the psalmist experiences the absence of God by recalling the temple liturgy (42:5). On another level of consciousness confidence and hope grow as the poet anticipates the presence of God, that is, the light and fidelity of God that will usher him into his presence (43:3). The key problem remains the absence of God. Paradoxically, however, God is present through his absence, an absence felt in the very depths of one's being. As a result, it brings about anxiety and grief. Coupled with this pain are the taunts of the enemies that heighten the sense of God's presence through nostalgia.

The transition from disorientation to reorientation is observable in other ways. Liturgically there is a dramatic movement from past nostalgia for worship (42:5) to future participation in divine services (43:4). In terms of time there is a decided switch from the painful succession of day and night when tears are the psalmist's food (42:4) to the optimistic rhythm of day and night when he will sing of his covenant God's fidelity (42:9). In the nuances of the refrain mentioned above there is a noticeable transformation. In 42:6 the voice is timid and stifled. In 42:12 it is affirmative yet reproachful. In 43:5 it is triumphant and victorious.

At prayer we also yearn for a sign of God's presence, something concrete that will show that he is there. Deep within we acknowledge that our move from disorientation (death, disease, unemployment, falling out of love, rejection by friends, etc.) to reorientation is fundamentally a move from the absence to the presence of God. Prayer is that paradoxical moment when the disconcerting facts of our disorientation evoke past divine presence and make us press on for newer presence. Prayer is that occasion when the hope of the chief refrain of this psalm exhorts us to leave the old behind and accept the new. It is a time when we confess our limited human resources and thereby no longer hope in them but in our God. Reorientation is the embrace of the all-powerful God and the farewell to our self-centered forces.

Presence makes the heart grow fonder. Because of covenant involvement, we are called upon to make our experience of God's presence at prayer, especially at liturgy, the basis of hope for others. To know God's presence in these settings is to be aware of his seeming absence in other situations, such as those of broken humans who long for presence but do not feel capable of even articulating that longing. Merely to stand beside an alienated human is to symbolize the contagious dimension of prayer. To hear the Word proclaimed and to share in Eucharist imply moving from the sanctuary to the hospital, nursing home, jail, and so on. Prayer is not the occasion for an egotistical hoarding of God's presence. Prayer is the moment for our altruistic overcoming of God's absence. Prayer is to be the assault on the disorientation of others whereby they will be moved to sing, "Wait for God, for I shall again praise him, / my savior and my God."

## Psalm 51
### The Miserere: Prayer of Repentance

[1]For the leader. A psalm of David, [2]when Nathan the prophet came to him after he had gone in to Bathsheba.

I

[3]Have mercy on me, God, in accord with your merciful love;
   in your abundant compassion blot out my transgressions.
[4]Thoroughly wash away my guilt;
   and from my sin cleanse me.
[5]For I know my transgressions;
   my sin is always before me.
[6]Against you, you alone have I sinned;
   I have done what is evil in your eyes
So that you are just in your word,
   and without reproach in your judgment.
[7]Behold, I was born in guilt,
   in sin my mother conceived me.
[8]Behold, you desire true sincerity;
   and secretly you teach me wisdom.
[9]Cleanse me with hyssop, that I may be pure;
   wash me, and I will be whiter than snow.
[10]You will let me hear gladness and joy;
   the bones you have crushed will rejoice.

II

[11]Turn away your face from my sins;
   blot out all my iniquities.
[12]A clean heart create for me, God;
   renew within me a steadfast spirit.
[13]Do not drive me from before your face,
   nor take from me your holy spirit.

<sup>14</sup>Restore to me the gladness of your salvation;
    uphold me with a willing spirit.
<sup>15</sup>I will teach the wicked your ways,
    that sinners may return to you.
<sup>16</sup>Rescue me from violent bloodshed, God, my saving God,
    and my tongue will sing joyfully of your justice.
<sup>17</sup>Lord, you will open my lips;
    and my mouth will proclaim your praise.
<sup>18</sup>For you do not desire sacrifice or I would give it;
    a burnt offering you would not accept.
<sup>19</sup>My sacrifice, O God, is a contrite spirit;
    a contrite, humbled heart, O God, you will not scorn.

III

<sup>20</sup>Treat Zion kindly according to your good will;
    build up the walls of Jerusalem.
<sup>21</sup>Then you will desire the sacrifices of the just,
    burnt offering and whole offerings;
    then they will offer up young bulls on your altar.

This psalm, known as the *Miserere* from the opening word of the ancient Latin translation, is one of the best known psalms. (It is also one of the seven penitential psalms—see Ps 32.) For the process leading from disorientation to reorientation this poem is extremely useful. It reveals the very personal nature of sin as a disruption of relationships, not only among humans, but also between God and the individual. It also describes reorientation in terms of cleansing and restoration. It may be divided as follows: (1) prayer for pardon and acknowledgment of sin (vv. 3-9); (2) prayer for restoration (vv. 10-14); (3) praise of God in the presence of the community and the sacrifice of a humbled heart (vv. 15-19); (4) prayer for the reconstruction of Jerusalem and restoration of temple worship (vv. 20-21).

The psalmist uses three different Hebrew words for "sin" in this piece. The first (*ḥṭ'*) is translated "sin" or "sinner." It implies the failure of the person to carry out an obligation concerning God. In verses 4 and 9 sin is that distortion of the relationship with God that demands cleansing. In verse 6 the psalmist announces that he has missed the mark on a very personal level: "Against you, you alone have I sinned." In verse 7 he observes that there never was a time in his life without sin. Finally in verse 11 he asks God to turn away his face from his sins and thereby grant peace and forgiveness.

The second word for "sin" (*pš*) is translated "transgression." This term connotes rebellion and revolt. In verse 3 the psalmist appeals to God's compassion to blot out his rebellious action. In verse 5 he honestly attests to the personal nature of this revolt: "For I know my transgressions." On the positive side the rebellious psalmist can use this experience to lead other rebels back to God: "I will teach the wicked your ways" (v. 15).

A third word for "sin" (*'wn*) is translated "guilt" or "guilty." As a deeply religious term, it indicates moral guilt or iniquity in God's sight. In verse 4 the psalmist parallels the washing away of guilt with cleansing from sin. In verse 7 he also parallels guilt at the moment of birth with sin at the moment of conception. Like sin, guilt is an omnipresent reality for the psalmist. It is only natural for him to beg God to blot out this state.

By a variety of Hebrew words the psalmist captures the cleansing needed for reorientation. Using a word evoking the image of washing clothes in cold water, the psalmist asks God to wash him, making him "whiter than snow" (v. 9). Employing a term recalling ritual purification (see Lev 13:17), the writer wants God to cleanse him of his sin (v. 4). In verse 9 the result of God's intervention is that the psalmist will be pure. Finally, taking advantage of a word connoting cleansing through ritual and sacrifice (see Num 19:19), the psalmist prays, "Cleanse me with hyssop" (v. 9). (Hyssop was an aromatic bush with many wooden twigs that functioned as a sprinkler in rites of cleansing—see Lev 14:4; Num 19:18.) The poet prays that God will thus reinstate him to the intimacy of his friendship and love.

Understanding the human person as a whole, the Hebrew Bible uses the terms "heart" and "spirit" with certain nuances. The "heart," meaning the mind and the will, is that center of the person from which activity and loyalty derive. "Spirit" (also translated "breath" and "wind") designates the total individual under the influence of God, open to God's plans, and willing to do God's will.

In verse 12 the psalmist acknowledges that the process of reorientation stems from God's action: "A clean heart *create* for me, God" (emphasis added). "Clean heart" envisions a purified self bent on a faithful course of action. In verse 19 there is mention of a "contrite, humbled heart." God will not despise one who through catastrophe has learned how to reorient his or her life for the future.

In verse 19 the psalmist has paralleled "a contrite spirit" with "a contrite, humbled heart." His sacrifice is the willingness to let God impact his future. In verse 12 he speaks of "a steadfast spirit" and in verse 14 of "a willing spirit." These phrases depict a person who after disaster seeks to enter upon a new manner of life. For this life God's action is paramount. Hence the psalmist prays in verse 13, "nor take from me your holy spirit." (For this entire process of ritual purification and renewal of the whole person, see Ezek 36:25-27.)

At prayer we cannot dismiss our own sinfulness out of hand. In light of Psalm 51 we must see sinfulness, not as a penalty for illegal activity, but as a personal affront to our God. The terms "rebellion" and "guilt" may help us to realize the intimate dimensions of sin. Since by sinning we also hurt our sisters and brothers, we must take steps to overcome the pain we have caused them. Covenant links our God and our community with our individual actions.

We also suffer intensely when another deliberately offends us. While we know we must offer that person forgiveness, we implicitly vow at times that hell will freeze over before we forgive. At prayer Psalm 51 urges us to acknowledge the broken spirit and heart of our offenders. We are bidden to be agents of restoration. To offer reconciliation is to continue God's work of creation. We must breathe the Spirit over the broken humanity of our sisters and brothers and thereby overcome the chaos of their lives. To pray Psalm 51 is to assume the ministry of reconciliation.

## Psalm 69
### A Cry of Anguish in Great Distress

[1]For the leader; according to "Lilies." Of David.

I

[2]Save me, God,
   for the waters have reached my neck.
[3]I have sunk into the mire of the deep,
   where there is no foothold.
I have gone down to the watery depths;
   the flood overwhelms me.

⁴I am weary with crying out;
    my throat is parched.
My eyes fail,
    from looking for my God.
⁵More numerous than the hairs of my head
    are those who hate me without cause.
Those who would destroy me are mighty,
    my enemies without reason.
Must I now restore
    what I did not steal?

II

⁶God, you know my folly;
    my faults are not hidden from you.
⁷Let those who wait in hope for you, LORD of hosts,
    not be shamed because of me.
Let those who seek you, God of Israel,
    not be disgraced because of me.
⁸For it is on your account I bear insult,
    that disgrace covers my face.
⁹I have become an outcast to my kindred,
    a stranger to my mother's children.
¹⁰Because zeal for your house has consumed me,
    I am scorned by those who scorn you.
¹¹When I humbled my spirit with fasting,
    this led only to scorn.
¹²When I clothed myself in sackcloth;
    I became a byword for them.
¹³Those who sit in the gate gossip about me;
    drunkards make me the butt of songs.

III

¹⁴But I will pray to you, LORD,
    at a favorable time.
God, in your abundant kindness, answer me
    with your sure deliverance.
¹⁵Rescue me from the mire,
    and do not let me sink.
Rescue me from those who hate me
    and from the watery depths.

¹⁶Do not let the flood waters overwhelm me,
    nor the deep swallow me,
    nor the pit close its mouth over me.
¹⁷Answer me, LORD, in your generous love;
    in your great mercy turn to me.
¹⁸Do not hide your face from your servant;
    hasten to answer me, for I am in distress.
¹⁹Come and redeem my life;
    because of my enemies ransom me.
²⁰You know my reproach, my shame, my disgrace;
    before you stand all my foes.
²¹Insult has broken my heart, and I despair;
    I looked for compassion, but there was none,
    for comforters, but found none.
²²Instead they gave me poison for my food;
    and for my thirst they gave me vinegar.

IV

²³May their own table be a snare for them,
    and their communion offerings a trap.
²⁴Make their eyes so dim they cannot see;
    keep their backs ever feeble.
²⁵Pour out your wrath upon them;
    let the fury of your anger overtake them.
²⁶Make their camp desolate,
    with none to dwell in their tents.
²⁷For they pursued the one you struck,
    added to the pain of the one you wounded.
²⁸Heap punishment upon their punishment;
    let them gain from you no vindication.
²⁹May they be blotted from the book of life;
    not registered among the just!

V

³⁰But here I am miserable and in pain;
    let your saving help protect me, God,
³¹That I may praise God's name in song
    and glorify it with thanksgiving.
³²That will please the LORD more than oxen,
    more than bulls with horns and hooves:

[33]"See, you lowly ones, and be glad;
   you who seek God, take heart!
[34]For the LORD hears the poor,
   and does not spurn those in bondage.
[35]Let the heaven and the earth praise him,
   the seas and whatever moves in them!"
VI
[36]For God will rescue Zion,
   and rebuild the cities of Judah.
They will dwell there and possess it;
   [37]the descendants of God's servants will inherit it;
   those who love God's name will dwell in it.

This lament is a graphic description of acute pain, faith in the Lord, and the desire for revenge. The psalmist seems to be seriously ill (vv. 27, 30), perhaps to the point of death (vv. 2-3). He is persecuted by enemies (v. 5) and smitten by God (vv. 9-10). The poem may be divided as follows: (1) cry for help (v. 2a); (2) lament (vv. 2b-5); (3) acknowledgment of wrongdoing (v. 6); (4) prayer (v. 7); (5) lament (vv. 8-13); (6) prayer (vv. 14-19); (7) lament (vv. 20-22); (8) curse against the enemy (vv. 23-29); (9) thanksgiving (vv. 30-35); (10) addition in the aftermath of the destruction of Jerusalem (vv. 36-37).

The poet paints a powerful picture of human dereliction. In verses 2b-3, 15-16 the psalmist depicts himself as being in Sheol, the underworld: mire, watery depths, flood. Sheol is more a state than a place. It is the state of being removed from God's concern and experiencing utter loneliness. Although the psalmist is not without sin (v. 6), still the present debacle is senseless. Indeed it is scandalous. The Lord's faithful people may be led to doubt their God because of the psalmist's unmitigated suffering (v. 7). But the irony of the situation is that this catastrophe is the result of serving the Lord. For the Lord's sake he bears insult (v. 8a); because of zeal for the Lord's house, he is scorned (v. 10). The disheartening reality is that the Lord is totally aware of his servant's condition (v. 20), yet apparently does not even lift a finger to help. Perhaps the pathos of the poem reaches its highest point in verse 21b, where the psalmist seeks pity and comfort only to find none (see Lam 1:2, 16-17, 21).

Verses 23-29, the psalmist's curse of the enemy, raise the problem of the cursing psalms in general (see, e.g., Pss 83:10-19; 109:5-20;

129:5-8) and the significance of these verses for the psalmist in particular. In their approach to prayer some people have recommended that these verses be eliminated from the church's official liturgical books or at least drastically truncated. Such people are naturally appalled by these vehement expressions of revenge and question their relevancy for prayer. Two questions seem to emerge: (1) what is the intent of these psalms? and (2) is there a place for anger in our prayer life?

Justice is the intent of these psalms. In the ancient Near East, where police forces and correctional institutions were nonexistent, the curse played a prominent role in the human quest for justice. These curses were solemn legal formulae. They were considered legally binding and rested on the sanction of the god upon whose will the entire social order depended. Essentially they were powerful demands that justice prevail by means of divine intervention. For the oppressed these curses were the way to redress injustice.

Anger occupies a legitimate place in our prayer life. Too often we have been seduced into thinking that emotion opposes reason. According to Israel's traditions the emotion brought about by the Hebrews' lament (see Exod 2:23-24) moves the Lord to act on behalf of his people. According to sound psychology we must reply to life's threats through anger. Anger thereby becomes a significant component in our human growth. To suppress anger does not contribute to an integral human life. According to covenant theology God's people have the right to express their grief in a community setting. The destructive tendencies of social evil are thus articulated in a form where the sufferers can hope for the bottoming out of disorientation. Ultimately anger does not necessarily stifle the human spirit since it is capable of rendering us yet more human.

At prayer we dare not hide or suppress the grief that overwhelms us. In seeking to move from disorientation to reorientation, we are encouraged after the manner of Psalm 69 not only to speak out but also to become angry. Our predecessors in this endeavor are, in chronological and ascending order, Moses (see Num 11:1–12:16; 20:2-13), Jeremiah (see Jer 11:18-23; 12:1-6; 17:12-18), and Jesus (see Mark 15:21-39). No one would suggest that their prayer was faulty or disrespectful. In communing with this God, we are urged to follow these intrepid examples of biblical tradition. Ours is not a God who advises us to utter only churchy prayers. Ours is not a God who recommends that we speak the polite language of manuals of devotion. Ours is a God who wants his presence recognized even if the only way of acknowledging that presence is the raw speech of angry laments.

At prayer, even our most intimate prayer, we must hear the laments of others who are empowered to overcome our insensitivity by their rightful demand for social justice. We are challenged by this psalm to undo the plight of the psalmist for our audience. We are asked to comfort the comfortless and pity the pitiless (see v. 21). We are furthermore challenged to bring to public attention the anger that has been suppressed and the anxiety that has been denied. Prayer must mean that the unexpressed fears and frustrations of our sisters and brothers will come to the surface so that they will no longer sink in the mire (vv. 3, 15) or be overwhelmed by the deep waters (vv. 3, 15). By such prayer we will understand the angry Jesus who pronounced curses on those who did not provide for the hungry, the thirsty, the strangers, the naked, and the imprisoned (see Matt 25:41-45).

## Psalm 44
### God's Past Favor and Israel's Present Need

¹For the leader. A *maskil* of the Korahites.

I

²O God, we have heard with our own ears;
    our ancestors have told us
The deeds you did in their days,
    with your own hand in days of old:
³You rooted out nations to plant them,
    crushed peoples and expelled them.
⁴Not with their own swords did they conquer the land,
    nor did their own arms bring victory;
It was your right hand, your own arm,
    the light of your face for you favored them.
⁵You are my king and my God,
    who bestows victories on Jacob.
⁶Through you we batter our foes;
    through your name we trample our adversaries.
⁷Not in my bow do I trust,
    nor does my sword bring me victory.

⁸You have brought us victory over our enemies,
  shamed those who hate us.
⁹In God we have boasted all the day long;
  your name we will praise forever.

*Selah*

II
¹⁰But now you have rejected and disgraced us;
  you do not march out with our armies.
¹¹You make us retreat before the foe;
  those who hate us plunder us at will.
¹²You hand us over like sheep to be slaughtered,
  scatter us among the nations.
¹³You sell your people for nothing;
  you make no profit from their sale.
¹⁴You make us the reproach of our neighbors,
  the mockery and scorn of those around us.
¹⁵You make us a byword among the nations;
  the peoples shake their heads at us.
¹⁶All day long my disgrace is before me;
  shame has covered my face
¹⁷At the sound of those who taunt and revile,
  at the sight of the enemy and avenger.
III
¹⁸All this has come upon us,
  though we have not forgotten you,
  nor been disloyal to your covenant.
¹⁹Our hearts have not turned back,
  nor have our steps strayed from your path.
²⁰Yet you have left us crushed,
  desolate in a place of jackals;
  you have covered us with a shadow of death.
²¹If we had forgotten the name of our God,
  stretched out our hands to another god,
²²Would not God have discovered this,
  God who knows the secrets of the heart?
²³For you we are slain all the day long,
  considered only as sheep to be slaughtered.

IV

<sup>24</sup>Awake! Why do you sleep, O Lord?
   Rise up! Do not reject us forever!
<sup>25</sup>Why do you hide your face;
   why forget our pain and misery?
<sup>26</sup>For our soul has been humiliated in the dust;
   our belly is pressed to the earth.
<sup>27</sup>Rise up, help us!
   Redeem us in your mercy.

In this communal lament Israel probes the apparent absence of God. The distance between her creedal formulations of the Lord's fidelity and the present state of affairs threatens to become an ever-widening chasm with theology on one side and history on the other. The psalm reflects some national catastrophe, although one cannot be specific as to the precise event. As part of the book of Psalms, this poem also transcends its original setting to offer a model for coping with the Lord's apparent aloofness. It may be divided as follows: (1) recitation of the Lord's past record of fidelity (vv. 2-4); (2) trust as Israel's expected response (vv. 5-9); (3) vivid description of the present impasse (vv. 10-17); (4) protestations of fidelity and trust (vv. 18-23); (5) bold demand for the Lord's immediate action (vv. 24-27).

The psalmist begins by focusing on the Lord's discriminatory holy war (see Ps 3) activities. In the past the Lord clearly distinguished between the enemy and Israel; he defeated the nations but granted victory to his own people (v. 3). The only response Israel made at that time was one of complete faith—military might was not needed (v. 4). In verses 5-9 the psalmist continues this holy war motif. Israel's victories were due to the Lord's exploits, a fact that Israel observed through a liturgy of praise (v. 9). However, in verses 10-17 the psalmist adopts a radically new tone because of the radically new state of affairs (note the word "But" in v. 10). The charge leveled against the Lord is that he is now practicing reverse discrimination. Whereas the Lord previously shamed the enemy (v. 8), he now shames his own people instead. The signs of the Lord's dereliction of duty are all too glaring: the enemy's plundering (v. 11), the dispersion of the prisoners in foreign countries (v. 12), the scorn and ridicule suffered by Israel (vv. 14-15). What adds insult to injury is the fact that the Lord has not even behaved like a good merchant. He did not receive anything resembling a reasonable price when he sold off his property (v. 13). Israel has unfortunately become the public example of divine impotence.

In verses 18-22 the people protest that their punishment is in no way commensurate with their behavior. They have abided by the terms of the covenant (v. 18) and have stayed the course asked of them (v. 19). Nonetheless jackals make their dwellings in the ruins of the gutted cities (v. 20). Surely this God must be aware of what is happening since nothing is hidden from him (vv. 21-22). The damnable reality is that Israel suffers this excruciating dilemma because of the Lord (v. 23).

In verses 24-27 Israel takes the only course of action left. The people demand that this lethargic God wake up and survey the situation (v. 24). They make the audacious request that the Lord become conspicuous by his presence, not his absence (v. 25). Here the psalmist contrasts two positions: Israel's groveling posture on the ground (v. 26) and the Lord's rising up as in the old days when he led their armies to victory (see Num 10:35). The psalm concludes on the only theological premise left to Israel: the Lord's covenant fidelity (v. 27: "mercy"). Though the devastation is enormous and the pain all too acute, still hope for the community resides, not in policies, plans, or programs, but in a Person. The Lord must research his faithful actions of the past so that he will be consistent in the present.

As a community at prayer, we must not hesitate to use the bold language of this psalm. In the face of nuclear or chemical warfare we must stir the Mighty Warrior to action. In view of the severe food shortages around the globe we must appeal to the maternal instincts of our God (see Ps 145) to feed her family. In the light of ongoing conflict around the world, we must move the King to effect peace in his domain. It is covenant that gives us the right to make such demands. Not to employ such bold language at prayer is to deny our status as a covenant community. We must not allow our God to sleep any longer! Disorientation is never desirable for its own sake.

Covenant is also calculated to make us reject our own lethargy in the midst of the evils that plague our sisters and brothers. Community prayer is the moment to rise to the occasion and allow our God to act through us. Community prayer is designed to empower us to work for the present liberation of fellow humans, not to sedate us with pondering our past noble deeds. Our God will be freed to act to the extent that we remove his shackles. In community prayer we learn—painfully, no doubt—that human presence can overcome divine absence. Ours is a God who not only trusts us but also needs us. At prayer we are urged not to abdicate the throne but to take our rightful place as kings and queens who hear the cries of the poor and then act. Community prayer is intended to teach us that our sisters and brothers have the right to impose on our sense of covenant loyalty so that the exodus from disorientation may begin.

## Psalm 58
## The Dethroning of Unjust Rulers

¹For the leader. Do not destroy. A *miktam* of David.
I
²Do you indeed pronounce justice, O gods;
    do you judge fairly you children of Adam?
³No, you freely engage in crime;
    your hands dispense violence to the earth.
II
⁴The wicked have been corrupt since birth;
    liars from the womb, they have gone astray.
⁵Their venom is like the venom of a snake,
    like that of a serpent stopping its ears,
⁶So as not to hear the voice of the charmer
    or the enchanter with cunning spells.
III
⁷O God, smash the teeth in their mouths;
    break the fangs of these lions, Lord!
⁸Make them vanish like water flowing away;
    trodden down, let them wither like grass.
⁹Let them dissolve like a snail that oozes away,
    like an untimely birth that never sees the sun.
¹⁰Suddenly, like brambles or thistles,
    have the whirlwind snatch them away.
¹¹Then the just shall rejoice to see the vengeance
    and bathe their feet in the blood of the wicked.
¹²Then people will say:
    "Truly there is a reward for the just;
    there is a God who is judge on earth!"

The original setting of this psalm was perhaps the divine tribunal of the Canaanite pantheon (the gods and goddesses of the pre-Israelite inhabitants of the Promised Land). (A "miktam" is probably a literary or musical term.) In this scenario the chief god El charges the other gods (v. 2: "O gods") with unjust judgments on earth. This exemplifies the typical wisdom tradition of establishing a just order on earth. In its Israelite form, however, the psalm is a communal lament in which the petitioner places himself among the wronged. It thus becomes a prophetic denunciation (see, e.g., Hos 4:1-3) with a request for the punishment of the wrongdoers. It may be divided as follows: (1) appeal (v. 2); (2) denunciation of the crimes (vv. 3-6); (3) petition for punishment (vv. 7-10); (4) conclusion (vv. 11-12).

In denouncing the crime the psalmist proceeds in a general way; he does not offer a concrete report of specific crimes. Similarly the guilty form a group—they are not singled out as individuals. This suggests the danger whereby the powerful, as they prefer, will remain anonymous as they perpetrate their crimes. The snake (vv. 5-6) plays a key role in the poetic development of the theme. The psalmist so portrays the snake that it expresses the very manifestation of evil. Hence the psalm deals with evil as such, not a particular instance of some concrete act of injustice.

In verses 7-10 the psalmist appeals to God's justice in maintaining the order in the world. Hence he utters curses whose fulfillment, namely, the utter destruction of the evildoers, will restore the balance. When the Lord acts upon these petitions, the just will rejoice as they "bathe their feet in the blood of the wicked" (v. 11). God's response will bear eloquent witness to his sense of justice.

In community prayer we must acknowledge the disorientation of injustice. The perversion of justice in whatever form contributes to the breakdown of balance and harmony. In view of the violence inflicted by the powerful we must adopt the passionate language of Psalm 58. At prayer our task is not to foment violence but to urge our God to restore justice. To thirst for justice (see Matt 5:6) is to thirst for the just God.

If our communal prayer is not to be a petition for the reign of justice only in heaven, then it must help to establish that reign here on earth. Such prayer is the setting for posing questions such as these: Who are those who practice injustice? Where is the modern snake? How does it

operate? Our communal prayer must result in the conviction that whenever people experience injustice and violence (hence disorientation), we
all experience injustice and violence (hence disorientation). Such prayer,
if it is to promote the move to reorientation, must insist more on our
obligations than our rights. Prayer is that disturbing encounter when
we push aside the question "what can you do for us?" to dwell on "what
must we do for you?" To pray to this covenant God is to commit our
community to the needs of all his children. Justice is simply the acknowledgment that we no longer regard disorientation as the ordinary state
of our sisters and brothers. The abuse of power in both our church and
society at large can never be standard business procedure.

### Psalm 85
### Prayer for Divine Favor

¹For the leader. A psalm of the Korahites.

I

²You once favored, LORD, your land,
    restored the captives of Jacob.
³You forgave the guilt of your people,
    pardoned all their sins.

*Selah*

⁴You withdrew all your wrath,
    turned back from your burning anger.

II

⁵Restore us, God of our salvation;
    let go of your displeasure with us.
⁶Will you be angry with us forever,
    prolong your anger for all generations?
⁷Certainly you will again restore our life,
    that your people may rejoice in you.
⁸Show us, LORD, your mercy;
    grant us your salvation.

III

⁹I will listen for what God, the LORD, has to say;
    surely he will speak of peace
To his people and to his faithful.
    May they not turn to foolishness!

¹⁰Near indeed is his salvation for those who fear him;
    glory will dwell in our land.
¹¹Love and truth will meet;
    justice and peace will kiss.
¹²Truth will spring from the earth;
    justice will look down from heaven.
¹³Yes, the LORD will grant his bounty;
    our land will yield its produce.
¹⁴Justice will march before him,
    and make a way for his footsteps.

As a lament, this psalm lacks the pathos of Psalm 69 and the despondent note of Psalm 44. While it focuses on Israel's problem, it accentuates the type of response expected of God's people. It is a meditation on the meaning of peace and the manner of acquiring it. Although it perhaps originally depicted the exile, within the book of Psalms it takes on wider meaning by suggesting the program of peace in other situations of dire need. It may be divided as follows: (1) previous experience of grace (vv. 2-4); (2) request for renewal and return from exile (vv. 5-8); (3) oracle of salvation (vv. 9-10); (4) covenant renewal (vv. 11-14).

In the first section (vv. 2-4) the psalmist offers a solid reason for Israel's hope: the Lord has acted favorably in the past. Not surprisingly, the land motif appears (v. 2), since peace obviously has something to do with the land. In previous times of upheaval and disruption the Lord placed greater emphasis on grace than his "burning anger" (v. 4). This recollection now prompts the people's plea: restoration (v. 5), overcoming divine wrath (v. 6), renewal as the setting for praise (v. 7), and the positive demonstration of covenant concern (v. 8).

At this point the psalmist puts aside any recital of the Lord's past saving deeds. He simply pronounces a prophetic oracle assuring peace because the God of Israel is ever with his people (vv. 9-10). It is significant, however, that God's presence is bound up with the people's fidelity (v. 9). At issue, therefore, are both God's gift and human response. God's gift-giving and human response are components in this relationship. However, while the psalmist does not resolve the tension between divine gift and human reward, he may imply that we are more comfortable with our own efforts than with God's gift.

In the last section (vv. 11-14) the psalmist resumes the land theme of verse 2. Verse 13 can create the impression that peace consists only in the absence of violence and the presence of material prosperity. However, the covenant vocabulary in this section assures us that our impression is inadequate. "Truth" (vv. 11a, 12a) implies total dedication. "Justice" (vv. 11b, 12b) means proper order, and hence, peace. When we have the union of love and truth and of truth and justice, we have genuine harmony between God and his people.

At community prayer we must dwell on God's call and our response. In order to achieve peace in the aftermath of disorientation we must express our willingness to accept this God and reject all those false idols that detract from covenant union. To overcome disorientation as a community, we must open ourselves to the point of being totally grounded in this Lord. Community prayer means, therefore, the dismantling of our anxieties, doubts, and despair. Reorientation is the embrace of realism: the acceptance of the covenant God and his demands. Life based on false goals and preoccupations can only result in greater alienation. Community prayer basically means renewing the terms of our community life: life with this God and his people.

Community prayer is the time for pronouncing oracles. In and through prayer our God charges us as a community to proclaim the message of peace to our world. This implies alerting people to the powers of oppression and empowering them to dare to hope again—a task that involves a theology of revelation. Revelation and prayer unmask the false values that tend to usurp the place of our God (power, violence, unbridled ambition, etc.). They present the true values that announce the abiding presence of our God (justice, compassion, love, etc.). In this way our world will yearn to be healed and so cope with disorientation. It will also resist clutching a self-centered past and thus move on to reorientation. Prayer is the setting in motion of the plan of peace: harmony between God and humans, harmony among humans, and harmony between humans and the world of nature. Prayer assures us that this vision is no utopia.

## Psalm 90
## God's Eternity and Human Frailty

¹A prayer of Moses, the man of God.

I

Lord, you have been our refuge
through all generations.
²Before the mountains were born,
the earth and the world brought forth,
from eternity to eternity you are God.
³You turn humanity back into dust,
saying, "Return, you children of Adam!"
⁴A thousand years in your eyes
are merely a day gone by,
Before a watch passes in the night,
⁵you wash them away;
They sleep,
and in the morning they sprout again like an herb.
⁶In the morning it blooms only to pass away;
in the evening it is wilted and withered.

II

⁷Truly we are consumed by your anger,
filled with terror by your wrath.
⁸You have kept our faults before you,
our hidden sins in the light of your face.
⁹Our life ebbs away under your wrath;
our years end like a sigh.
¹⁰Seventy is the sum of our years,
or eighty, if we are strong;
Most of them are toil and sorrow;
they pass quickly, and we are gone.
¹¹Who comprehends the strength of your anger?
Your wrath matches the fear it inspires.
¹²Teach us to count our days aright,
that we may gain wisdom of heart.

III

¹³Relent, O LORD! How long?
Have pity on your servants!

$^{14}$Fill us at daybreak with your mercy,
   that all our days we may sing for joy.
$^{15}$Make us glad as many days as you humbled us,
   for as many years as we have seen trouble.
$^{16}$Show your deeds to your servants,
   your glory to their children.
$^{17}$May the favor of the Lord our God be ours.
   Prosper the work of our hands!
   Prosper the work of our hands!

This communal lament recited by an individual does not provide any specific background. Perhaps it is a meditation on human life in the light of God, concluding with a petition. Perhaps an old man reflects on human life and, pursuing God's eternity, begins to grasp the nature of that life. The poem may be divided as follows: (1) contrast between human duration and divine eternity (vv. 1-6); (2) consciousness of divine anger because of human sinfulness (vv. 7-11); (3) petitions for coping in life (vv. 12-17). Thus up to verse 11 there is a descent from the sadness of mortality to the tragedy of sin and divine anger. However, with verse 12 there is an ascent to the point of both accepting and coping.

In the first section (vv. 1-6) the psalmist begins with a recollection of God's help and assistance in the past that is at the same time an appeal for help and assistance in the present. The poet's use of "refuge" (v. 1) immediately conjures up the image of something stable. Against the background of God's eternity (v. 2) the human condition is anything but stable. Borrowing from the traditions of Genesis 2–3 the psalmist insists on the frailty of humans (v. 3). Time, moreover, is really on God's side: a thousand years is a mere nothing. While God is eternal, humans experience vitality only to see it instantly elude them (vv. 4-6).

Human sinfulness makes human life all the more difficult. Israel's God is not an impersonal force or energy. Rather, the Lord is truly a person who is provoked to anger by Israel's sins (vv. 7, 9, 11). Humans reject life because they reject the Author of life by their sins. Even their "hidden sins" (v. 8) cannot evade the scrutiny of this totally involved God. Even if they should live to be seventy or eighty (an exaggeration given the human life span of the time), they experience only sorrow and toil (v. 10).

Finally in verse 12 dire reflection gives way to petition. "[W]isdom of heart" is basically the art of living and the ability to adapt to the realities of life. In seeking to live, Israel engages the Living One. His covenant presence (v. 14: "mercy") makes life not only tolerable but also enjoyable. Israel next prays that this God will compensate in proportion to the evil sustained (v. 15). In verse 16 the community seeks to reawaken its sense of God's past activity in the context of the needs of the present. Recalling such history offers the means to cope. Finally Israel asks God's blessing on their work (v. 17). Human work, affirmed by God, is evidence of divine goodness, shares in his power, and gives meaning and fullness to life.

At prayer the community is often the doubting community, the sinful community. Disorientation is not infrequently the result of all too limited wisdom. We tend to see life as the accumulation of goods, the heaping up of distinctions, and the solidity of our ego. Like the couple in Eden, we make ourselves the norm of conduct and reject the wisdom that resides in genuine living. The move from disorientation to reorientation begins by acknowledging that we must be caught up with God, not a program of action. Community prayer must also bring us to realize that our sinfulness cannot defeat our God and ironically may be the point of departure for wise living. Because of covenant, we can even demand that God's past activities on our behalf (v. 16) be recognized as the precedent for help here and now. Community prayer is an exercise in recommitting ourselves to the belief that God, our community, and individuals have to interact as healthy covenant partners. Wisdom, and hence the defeat of disorientation, is our renewed enthusiasm to live, not exist, to celebrate, not tolerate.

Community prayer must also be operation outreach for those who doubt about God, the community, and especially themselves. To pray this communal lament is to share its conviction with such people. The work and glorious power of our God (v. 16) must be the community's contribution to the despairing. Essentially our prayer must be to teach them wisdom for the delicate art of living. In the face of human doubts and human sinfulness we must nonetheless share a God who calls us to happiness, who offers us the gift of his covenant presence, and who interacts in our work. To crush disorientation is to strike a blow for healthy community life. Community prayer is a demanding enterprise.

## New Testament

### Mark 15:21-39

²¹They pressed into service a passer-by, Simon, a Cyrenian, who was coming in from the country, the father of Alexander and Rufus, to carry his cross.

**The Crucifixion.** ²²They brought him to the place of Golgotha (which is translated Place of the Skull). ²³They gave him wine drugged with myrrh, but he did not take it. ²⁴Then they crucified him and divided his garments by casting lots for them to see what each should take. ²⁵It was nine o'clock in the morning when they crucified him. ²⁶The inscription of the charge against him read, "The King of the Jews." ²⁷With him they crucified two revolutionaries, one on his right and one on his left. [²⁸] ²⁹Those passing by reviled him, shaking their heads and saying, "Aha! You who would destroy the temple and rebuild it in three days, ³⁰save yourself by coming down from the cross." ³¹Likewise the chief priests, with the scribes, mocked him among themselves and said, "He saved others; he cannot save himself. ³²Let the Messiah, the King of Israel, come down now from the cross that we may see and believe." Those who were crucified with him also kept abusing him.

**The Death of Jesus.** ³³At noon darkness came over the whole land until three in the afternoon. ³⁴And at three o'clock Jesus cried out in a loud voice, "*Eloi, Eloi, lema sabachthani?*" which is translated, "My God, my God, why have you forsaken me?" ³⁵Some of the bystanders who heard it said, "Look, he is calling Elijah." ³⁶One of them ran, soaked a sponge with wine, put it on a reed, and gave it to him to drink, saying, "Wait, let us see if Elijah comes to take him down." ³⁷Jesus gave a loud cry and breathed his last. ³⁸The veil of the sanctuary was torn in two from top to bottom. ³⁹When the centurion who stood facing him saw how he breathed his last he said, "Truly this man was the Son of God!"

It is clear that Psalm 22 plays a central role in Mark's account of the suffering and death of Jesus. The dividing of the garments in 15:24 calls to mind, "they divide my garments among them; / for my clothing they cast lots" (v. 19). The jeering and the mockery of the chief priests in 15:31 reflect, "All who see me mock me; / they curl their lips and jeer; / they shake their heads at me. / 'He relied on the LORD—let him deliver him; / if he loves him, let him rescue him' (vv. 8-9). Jesus' cry of dereliction in 15:34 cites, "My God, my God, why have you abandoned me?" (v. 2). Whether or not Jesus actually uttered this saying is a matter of dispute. For some the cry from the cross is an authentic word of Jesus. For others the evidence for an authentic word is insufficient. In any event, what is clear is Mark's understanding of the mystery of the cross.

According to Mark Jesus comes to carry out his Father's plan. He is the Son of Man who chooses to "give his life as a ransom for many" (Mark 10:45). Such a Jesus is a suffering Son of Man whose relationship to the Father hinges on obedience. Suffering and obedience were traditional in Israel's laments. For Mark Jesus epitomizes the righteous sufferer in these psalms. However, Mark does not end his account with the suffering. The Father transforms the suffering into glory. The transition is from lament in suffering to praise of God's action. The thrust of the author of Psalm 22 comes to supreme expression in Jesus.

Disorientation is all too evident in Jesus' experience of pain and frustration. The cry of dereliction is the prayer of lament that the Father now makes Jesus' problem his problem. On the other hand, the reality of the cross is that Jesus must make the Father's problem his problem— he must achieve redemption through his suffering and death. Thus Jesus is bidden to let go, to relinquish the old securities, to accept the paradox of Calvary. Reorientation is the embrace of the Father at Easter. The resurrection is the clearest sign that Jesus is on a new level of being.

### Second Corinthians 11:30–12:10

[30]If I must boast, I will boast of the things that show my weakness. [31]The God and Father of the Lord Jesus knows, he who is blessed forever, that I do not lie. [32]At Damascus, the governor under King Aretas guarded the city of Damascus, in order to seize me, [33]but I was lowered in a basket through a window in the wall and escaped his hands.

[1]I must boast; not that it is profitable, but I will go on to visions and revelations of the Lord. [2]I know someone in Christ who, fourteen years ago (whether in the body or out of the body

I do not know, God knows), was caught up to the third heaven. ³And I know that this person (whether in the body or out of the body I do not know, God knows) ⁴was caught up into Paradise and heard ineffable things, which no one may utter. ⁵About this person I will boast, but about myself I will not boast, except about my weaknesses. ⁶Although if I should wish to boast, I would not be foolish, for I would be telling the truth. But I refrain, so that no one may think more of me than what he sees in me or hears from me ⁷because of the abundance of the revelations. Therefore, that I might not become too elated, a thorn in the flesh was given to me, an angel of Satan, to beat me, to keep me from being too elated. ⁸Three times I begged the Lord about this, that it might leave me, ⁹but he said to me, "My grace is sufficient for you, for power is made perfect in weakness." I will rather boast most gladly of my weaknesses, in order that the power of Christ may dwell with me. ¹⁰Therefore, I am content with weaknesses, insults, hardships, persecutions, and constraints, for the sake of Christ; for when I am weak, then I am strong.

In Second Corinthians 11–12 Paul takes up his manner of ministry. Although the text is a letter and not a lament, it nevertheless suggests the thrust of lament in coping with weakness, a stance not unlike that in Mark's passion account.

In replying to his opponents, Paul states that he too can boast about his Jewish background (11:22), his labors (11:23-29), and his visions (12:1-4). However, Paul prefers a different approach, namely, boasting about his weaknesses: "If I must boast, I will boast of the things that show my weakness" (11:30). He takes the same stance in 12:5. For Paul, weakness is not merely a declaration about the present state of affairs. Rather, it has an intrinsic power to extricate a person from the incrustations of ego and to move one to look beyond oneself. Far from creating doubts about his ministry, weakness becomes the symbol of apostolic authority and legitimation. "Therefore, I am content with weaknesses . . . for the sake of Christ; for when I am weak, then I am strong" (12:10). Paul thus exemplifies the disorientation-reorientation process. By his willingness to let go, to relinquish the self-directed patterns of ministry, he is able to embrace Christ and the experience of the transforming power of the resurrection.

Paul's manner of thinking and acting flies in the face of our pragmatic business procedures. In applying for jobs, we do not notify the prospective employer about weaknesses and failures. We choose to dwell on our strengths and successes in the hope that they will win the position for us. It is so difficult to accept Paul's teaching that in weakness power reaches perfection (12:10). Too often we have conceived of our God as the Celestial Personnel Officer who peruses dossiers and makes final determinations based on them. At prayer Paul suggests that we focus on the weakness of the Crucified and in that way derive strength for our mission. For Paul there is no detour around Calvary in the faith approach to overcoming disorientation. Paul was clearly in touch with his biblical traditions, with the lament as model for prayer and ministry.

## Summary of the theology of the laments

1. The laments, both individual and communal, are a school of prayer. They demand that we meet life head-on and thereby avoid the role of faking and making-believe.
2. We are bidden to let go of the securities of the past and see the dangers of the present not simply as a crisis but as a faith opportunity. Hence our situation can mean growth, not demise.
3. The laments are a study in human weakness. We are asked to look beyond ourselves to a generous God who creates us in the image of his Son, that is, as weak humans.
4. We are invited to see the weaknesses inherent in our ministry and make them the vehicle for God's presence. To cope with tragedy and pain is to announce that we do not travel by ourselves.
5. The lament of Jesus demands that we open ourselves up to the larger contours of our God's world of concern. We are forcefully reminded that covenant is a two-edged sword. By asking for help in our world of frustration, we implicitly commit ourselves to offering help in our God's world of frustration, namely, other people. To cry for help means to be willing to hear the community's cry for help.

# CHAPTER 7

# To a God of Surprises
## The Psalms of Declarative Praise

### *Surprise versus control*

The rumor has been verified: most of us do not like to be surprised. To be surprised implies that we have surrendered at least some of our autonomy—an event has occurred over which we have exercised little or no control. To be surprised further suggests that other people are invading the sacred domain of our independence. As a result, we program ourselves to eliminate all vestiges of surprise. When an apparent surprise does occur, we offer the explanation that we had a remote hand in its making. Hence it is not really a surprise at all.

We prefer to operate on the basis of checks and balances, cause and effect, energy expended and results obtained. In our ledgers everything must balance out. Otherwise we run the risk of distorting our prefabricated harmony. Therefore, we choose to focus on the things that we produce or manufacture. We find it exceedingly difficult to dwell on things that have not come off our assembly line. We dare not appreciate sunsets or symphonies because we would thereby admit that we did not produce them. And yet they are there yearning to be enjoyed, not merely stored away in the indifferent memory bank of our computers.

If somehow we get to the point where we can be surprised by things, we remain on principle opposed to being surprised by humans. They are not calculated, we think, to demonstrate the creativity of our God. Hence they dare not surprise us by their goodness. To offset this remote possibility, we reduce people to things, objects ready to provide us with instant pleasure, should the need arise. In our obsession we are precluded from asking these types of questions: In what way do these people reflect the Creator's image? How warm is their love and how great is their compassion? We do not want to be surprised because the truly human qualities of others will reveal our own selfishness and shallowness.

We are suffering from the demise of celebration. We have lost the radical ability to party, to have a good time. Hand in hand with our loss of celebration goes our loss of the sense of mystery. We do not want to celebrate the attainments of others because we have already labeled them as unproductive. It is painful to congratulate others because we choose not to break free from our ego-incarcerated world. To celebrate and congratulate would demand a new vision of reality.

At prayer we are challenged to believe in a God of surprises and indeed a God who surprises us through others. The breakthrough from disorientation to reorientation is in the nature of gift or grace. To pray to this God is to put aside our efforts at control. To pray to this God is to admit amazement and bewilderment that stem from Another and are not the result of our human efforts. This God is a God of surprises who invites us to marvel at his manifold gifts. The move from disorientation to reorientation occurs by way of gift-giving. And such gift-giving demands that we recover our sense of celebration. At prayer we must recapture for ourselves the truth that this God is a God who likes parties because it is the nature of this God to give.

## Thanksgivings or psalms of declarative praise

In the Hebrew Bible the verb "to thank" means "to praise." Hence it is not necessarily an expression of indebtedness for the granting of a request. While thanksgivings or psalms of declarative praise offer praise to God, they are distinct from hymns or psalms of descriptive praise (see chap. 2). Thanksgivings or psalms of declarative praise assert the presence of newness, not God's ongoing care for the world and humans. They are the expression of a person's specific experience of the Lord. Thus a communal thanksgiving or communal psalm of declarative praise offers the people's praise for something concrete that must find expression in worship. The focus of that worship is a God of surprises, not an ancient Near Eastern god of stability.

The structure of the thanksgiving or psalm of declarative praise (also called a psalm of narrative praise) normally consists of three elements: (1) introduction or call to praise; (2) account of the newness that the Lord has brought forth; (3) conclusion that is usually a renewed call to praise.

## Psalm 30
## Thanksgiving for Deliverance

¹A psalm. A song for the dedication of the Temple. Of David.

I

²I praise you, LORD, for you raised me up
    and did not let my enemies rejoice over me.
³O LORD, my God,
    I cried out to you for help and you healed me.
⁴LORD, you brought my soul up from Sheol;
    you let me live, from going down to the pit.

II

⁵Sing praise to the LORD, you faithful;
    give thanks to his holy memory.
⁶For his anger lasts but a moment;
    his favor a lifetime.
At dusk weeping comes for the night;
    but at dawn there is rejoicing.

III

⁷Complacent, I once said,
    "I shall never be shaken."
⁸LORD, you showed me favor,
    established for me mountains of virtue.
But when you hid your face
    I was struck with terror.
⁹To you, LORD, I cried out;
    with the Lord I pleaded for mercy:
¹⁰"What gain is there from my lifeblood,
    from my going down to the grave?

Does dust give you thanks
    or declare your faithfulness?
[11]Hear, O Lord, have mercy on me;
    Lord, be my helper."
IV
[12]You changed my mourning into dancing;
    you took off my sackcloth
    and clothed me with gladness.
[13]So that my glory may praise you
    and not be silent.
O Lord, my God,
    forever will I give you thanks.

This psalm of declarative praise is an individual's expression of divine deliverance from suffering and distress. The psalm may be divided as follows: (1) praise of the Lord for his intervention (v. 2); (2) recounting of the psalmist's experience (vv. 3-4); (3) invitation to those present to praise the Lord and learn from the psalmist's experience (vv. 5-6); (4) more explicit description of the problem (vv. 7-12); (5) conclusion (v. 13).

The artistry of the poet consists, not in simple repetition, but in the development of new elements as the psalm progresses. Verse 2 speaks of the psalmist's liberation. In verse 3a the psalmist cries out for help. In verses 3b-4 he experiences liberation: he was healed and brought up from the netherworld, Sheol. Then in verses 5-6 he takes up the theme of thanksgiving, calling upon the bystanders to take up the chorus of praise and learn from his experience. God's graciousness must be celebrated. At this point the psalmist introduces a new element in the supplication-liberation-thanksgiving schema: the fall. In verses 7-8 the psalmist mentions that he was overconfident and that he was consequently stricken with some distress. In verses 9-11 he takes up the supplication again, noting that the Lord would gain nothing from his death. In verse 12 he develops the liberation by speaking of the giftedness of the new situation. The removal of sackcloth and the dancing are evidence of reorientation. Finally in verse 13 he once again accentuates the duty of thanksgiving: abrupt newness must be communicated.

There are two opposite movements that govern the psalm, namely, life and death. In verses 4b and 10a death is symbolized by going down (into the pit or Sheol). In verses 6b and 10b death is symbolized by silence (weeping and the absence of praise). In verse 4a life is described in terms of bringing up and in verse 3a in terms of healing. In verses 2a, 5, 6b, and 13 the silence of death is vanquished by singing. In this psalm there is an ascending movement from (1) death to life, (2) sickness to health, (3) punishment (God's hidden face in v. 8b) to joy, and (4) night to morning (v. 6b).

At prayer we sometimes take uncanny delight in preferring death to life, sickness to health, punishment to joy, night to morning. The great failures are always before our eyes: alcoholism, drug addiction, consumerism, and so forth. All too easily they remind us of the psalmist: "Complacent, I once said, / 'I shall never be shaken.' . . . But when you hid your face / I was struck with terror" (vv. 7-8). Prayer, however, must challenge us to reflect on life, health, joy, and morning. We are asked to remember the rehabilitated and the reformed—ample proof that there is indeed a God of surprises. We must hear their testimony, applaud their efforts, and share in the happiness of their reorientation. Why must we prefer sackcloth to dancing shoes (v. 12)? According to this psalm we must overcome our unwillingness to break out in praise.

Prayer must also turn us in the direction of those who still yearn for reorientation but have not yet achieved it. Why should death have the last word (v. 10)? In the context of covenant they cry out to us, "be my helper" (v. 11). The God of surprises truly deserves that title when he enlists humans in this enterprise of mutual help. The distressing question at prayer must be, After the cry for help, who will be the source of healing (v. 3)? To the extent that others experience misery, we are in Sheol, the pit. Our celebration of reorientation in the Father's raising of Jesus by sending the Spirit must lead us to make hope possible for the less-than-beautiful people. Insofar as we remove them from Sheol, the pit, we can join in Paul's celebrative chorus: "Death is swallowed up in victory. / Where, O death, is your victory? / Where, O death, is your sting?" (1 Cor 15:54-55).

## Psalm 40
### Gratitude and Prayer for Help

[1]For the leader. A psalm of David.

A
[2]Surely, I wait for the LORD;
     who bends down to me and hears my cry,

³Draws me up from the pit of destruction,
    out of the muddy clay,
Sets my feet upon rock,
    steadies my steps,
⁴And puts a new song in my mouth,
    a hymn to our God.
Many shall look on in fear
    and they shall trust in the LORD.
⁵Blessed the man who sets
    his security in the LORD,
    who turns not to the arrogant
    or to those who stray after falsehood.
⁶You, yes you, O LORD, my God,
    have done many wondrous deeds!
And in your plans for us
    there is none to equal you.
Should I wish to declare or tell them,
    too many are they to recount.
⁷Sacrifice and offering you do not want;
    you opened my ears.
Holocaust and sin-offering you do not request;
    ⁸so I said, "See; I come
    with an inscribed scroll written upon me.
⁹I delight to do your will, my God;
    your law is in my inner being!"
¹⁰When I sing of your righteousness
    in a great assembly,
See, I do not restrain my lips;
    as you, LORD, know.
¹¹I do not conceal your righteousness
    within my heart;
I speak of your loyalty and your salvation.
    I do not hide your mercy or faithfulness from a great
    assembly.
¹²LORD, may you not withhold
    your compassion from me;
May your mercy and your faithfulness
    continually protect me.

B
<sup>13</sup>But evils surround me
   until they cannot be counted.
My sins overtake me,
   so that I can no longer see.
They are more numerous than the hairs of my head;
   my courage fails me.
<sup>14</sup>Lord, graciously rescue me!
   Come quickly to help me, Lord!
<sup>15</sup>May those who seek to destroy my life
   be shamed and confounded.
Turn back in disgrace
   those who desire my ruin.
<sup>16</sup>Let those who say to me "Aha!"
   Be made desolate on account of their shame.
<sup>17</sup>While those who seek you
   rejoice and be glad in you.
May those who long for your salvation
   always say, "The Lord is great."
<sup>18</sup>Though I am afflicted and poor,
   my Lord keeps me in mind.
You are my help and deliverer;
   my God, do not delay!

This psalm initially strikes us as being odd. After the joyful mood of the thanksgiving in verses 2-12, there is an apparently unjustified switch to the somber mood of the lament in verses 13-18. Even within the thanksgiving the teaching about true sacrifice (vv. 7-9) seems to impede the psalmist's praise of the Lord in verses 6 and 10. To make matters worse, verses 14-18 are repeated with only slight variations in Psalm 70. While there is a probable explanation of the present state of Psalm 40, we will focus on the thanksgiving in verses 2-12. It may be divided as follows: (1) introduction (v. 2); (2) account of the Lord's deliverance (vv. 3-4); (3) instruction and praise (vv. 5-6); (4) meaning of true sacrifice (vv. 7-9); (5) enthusiastic conclusion of the thanksgiving with a final petition (vv. 10-12).

In verses 2-3 the psalmist sings of release from death, perhaps from some serious illness. Here he contrasts the precariousness of his situation (v. 3: "pit of destruction . . . muddy clay") with divine security (v. 3: "Sets my feet upon rock, / steadies my steps"). This complete reversal leads into an expression of his new state—there is a new song in his mouth (v. 4). At this juncture there is a beatitude reflecting the desirable state of those who trust in the Lord (v. 5). The Lord is simply incomparable—it is impossible to praise him enough (v. 6).

In verses 7-9 the psalm echoes the nature of genuine sacrifice as reflected in Israel's prophets who inveighed against purely mechanical worship (see Isa 1:10-17; Hos 6:4-6; Amos 5:21-27; Mic 6:6-8). Without denigrating ritual (the setting is the sanctuary!), this section stresses the essence of sacrifice, namely, listening and acting in faith. The law in the psalmist's "inner being" (v. 9) smacks of Jeremiah's insistence on the new covenant (see Jer 31:31-34). In verses 10-11 the psalmist attests that the Lord's gracious disruption in his life has not been a miser's booty but the boon of the community. It is hardly surprising that he requests God's ongoing compassion in verse 12.

At prayer, especially liturgical prayer, we must be overwhelmed by a theology that links worship and communal concern. Liturgy cannot be our flight from the disorientation that daily attends our world. Liturgy must be the awareness of our God's presence that impels us to those people and those situations where our God's absence is most conspicuous. Liturgy must announce our resolution to bring about reorientation. Liturgy means a priority on involvement outside the place of worship.

This psalm also describes what the new life of reorientation should be. It includes trust in God alone (v. 4), openness to God's requests (vv. 6-8), and sharing with others the experience of this newness (vv. 9-10). Such experience must become contagious for others.

## Psalm 73
## The Trial of the Just

[1]A psalm of Asaph.
How good God is to the upright,
   to those who are pure of heart!

I

[2]But, as for me, my feet had almost stumbled;
   my steps had nearly slipped,

³Because I was envious of the arrogant
    when I saw the prosperity of the wicked.
⁴For they suffer no pain;
    their bodies are healthy and sleek.
⁵They are free of the burdens of life;
    they are not afflicted like others.
⁶Thus pride adorns them as a necklace;
    violence clothes them as a robe.
⁷Out of such blindness comes sin;
    evil thoughts flood their hearts.
⁸They scoff and spout their malice;
    from on high they utter threats.
⁹They set their mouths against the heavens,
    their tongues roam the earth.
¹⁰So my people turn to them
    and drink deeply of their words.
¹¹They say, "Does God really know?"
    "Does the Most High have any knowledge?"
¹²Such, then, are the wicked,
    always carefree, increasing their wealth.

II

¹³Is it in vain that I have kept my heart pure,
    washed my hands in innocence?
¹⁴For I am afflicted day after day,
    chastised every morning.
¹⁵Had I thought, "I will speak as they do,"
    I would have betrayed this generation of your children.
¹⁶Though I tried to understand all this,
    it was too difficult for me,
¹⁷Till I entered the sanctuary of God
    and came to understand their end.

III

¹⁸You set them, indeed, on a slippery road;
    you hurl them down to ruin.
¹⁹How suddenly they are devastated;
    utterly undone by disaster!
²⁰They are like a dream after waking, Lord,
    dismissed like shadows when you arise.

IV

²¹Since my heart was embittered
    and my soul deeply wounded,
²²I was stupid and could not understand;
    I was like a brute beast in your presence.
²³Yet I am always with you;
    you take hold of my right hand.
²⁴With your counsel you guide me,
    and at the end receive me with honor.
²⁵Whom else have I in the heavens?
    None beside you delights me on earth.
²⁶Though my flesh and my heart fail,
    God is the rock of my heart, my portion forever.
²⁷But those who are far from you perish;
    you destroy those unfaithful to you.
²⁸As for me, to be near God is my good,
    to make the Lord GOD my refuge.
I shall declare all your works
    in the gates of daughter Zion.

Although some scholars regard this poem as a wisdom psalm, it seems that its insistence on radical newness accounts for its place here as a thanksgiving or psalm of declarative praise. ("A psalm of Asaph" indicates that this work was composed in the tradition of Asaph, an ancestor of one of the prominent guilds of temple singers and musicians.) It may be divided as follows: (1) anticipated conclusion (v. 1); (2) the prosperity of the arrogant (vv. 2-12); (3) temptation and new perception (vv. 13-17); (4) fate of the wicked (vv. 18-22); (5) fate of the good (vv. 23-28).

After the anticipated conclusion (v. 1), the psalmist takes up the classical problem of retribution: the evil prosper while the good perish. This is clearly the poet's painful stage of disorientation. In verses 4-5 he emphasizes the good health of the wicked. In verses 6-7 he describes their presumptuouness and violence. In verses 8-9 he moves on to their innate scorn and derision. In verses 10-11 he speaks of the effect of these arrogant wicked on the believing Israelite. Instead of seeing the practices of the wicked as anticovenantal, the believer is hoodwinked, becoming a convert to their blasphemy. Verse 12 summarizes the psalmist's painfully acquired observation.

In verses 13-14 the psalmist candidly exposes his own temptation. He is tempted to regard his fidelity as utterly senseless. The torments tend to add conviction to the position of the arrogant wicked. But to have given in would have meant being unfaithful to Israel's faith (v. 15). His failure to understand (v. 16) was necessary so that he could open up to a new vision (v. 17). This is the moment of reorientation, for this vision is not his own achievement but a gift. It is significant that God nowhere speaks in the psalm. However, it is in the process of meditation that the psalmist discovers the personal presence of God.

In verses 18-22 the psalmist examines the real fate of the wicked and criticizes his earlier temptation. He perceives that evil will not have the last word. God does not sit idly by. He sets the wicked on a slippery path so that in a short time they will be utterly devastated (vv. 18-20). At this point the psalmist recalls his earlier frame of mind that made him like a "brute beast" (vv. 21-22). What is significant in this section is that the poet for the first time addresses the Lord as "you." This is the gift whereby he becomes aware of God's presence. He does not ponder a theological problem in solitude. Rather, he opens himself up to accept the gratuitous presence of God. Theological problems must be aired in community.

In the conclusion the poet develops his new level of being. The Lord holds him, guides him, and receives him with honor (vv. 23-24). There is really no one else who matters in heaven or on earth (v. 25). Regardless of what happens to his physical well-being, the Lord is his constant support (v. 26). In the concluding verses the poet contrasts distance from and nearness to God. It is this nearness that prompts him to share the Lord's gift-giving with others.

At prayer we must be willing to accept the presence of our God as a gift. The limitations that are often at the root of our disorientation need not add to that state by way of revolt or despair. Reorientation awakens us to the presence of Another who invites us to think in terms of persons, not problems. Prayer must lead us to accept the embrace of our God, not simply a substitute to control our intellectual and emotional imbalance. We must learn from the psalmist to bring our doubts and problems to prayer with the expectation of personal encounter.

Prayer must also be our support in seeking answers to the dangers of our planet that involve the exploitation of our sisters and brothers. Prayer is to be our catalyst for asking hard questions, even if the answers are not immediately forthcoming. Reorientation does not so much mean that we have resolved all problems, but that we have left behind the secure but false solutions of the past and in the presence of our God embark on a new venture of answers. While we are always the beneficiaries of the past, we must also be the pioneers of the future.

## Psalm 92
## A Hymn of Thanksgiving for God's Fidelity

¹A psalm. A sabbath song.

I
²It is good to give thanks to the LORD,
 to sing praise to your name, Most High,
³To proclaim your love at daybreak,
 your faithfulness in the night,
⁴With the ten-stringed harp,
 with melody upon the lyre.
⁵For you make me jubilant, LORD, by your deeds;
 at the works of your hands I shout for joy.

II
⁶How great are your works, LORD!
 How profound your designs!
⁷A senseless person cannot know this;
 a fool cannot comprehend.
⁸Though the wicked flourish like grass
 and all sinners thrive,
They are destined for eternal destruction;
 ⁹but you, LORD, are forever on high.
¹⁰Indeed your enemies, LORD,
 indeed your enemies shall perish;
 all sinners shall be scattered.

III
¹¹You have given me the strength of a wild ox;
 you have poured rich oil upon me.
¹²My eyes look with glee on my wicked enemies;
 my ears shall hear what happens to my wicked foes.
¹³The just shall flourish like the palm tree,
 shall grow like a cedar of Lebanon.

¹⁴Planted in the house of the LORD,
     they shall flourish in the courts of our God.
¹⁵They shall bear fruit even in old age,
     they will stay fresh and green,
¹⁶To proclaim: "The LORD is just;
     my rock, in whom there is no wrong."

Although some consider this a psalm of descriptive praise, it seems to be oriented more toward declarative praise. Verses 2-4 present the psalmist's testimony and encouragement to others to praise God. Verses 5, 11-12 recall God's gracious intervention on his behalf. Admittedly the specific situation of the psalmist is not clear, although verses 10-12 sound like a victory song. It may be divided as follows: (1) the psalmist's joy over the Lord's great works (vv. 2-5); (2) recompense of the wicked and the psalmist (vv. 6-12); (3) reward of the just (vv. 13-16).

In the first section (vv. 2-5) the poet sings of the appropriateness of praising God for his covenant fidelity (vv. 2-3). Instrumental music contributes significantly to the occasion (v. 4). The works of the Lord's hands (v. 5) connect with the second section (vv. 6-12—note "works" in v. 6). The wicked in verse 8 who are also the Lord's enemies (v. 10) are those whose lifestyle disrupts the community. However, by mentioning the Lord's presence "on high" (v. 9), the psalmist implies that God in his heavenly realm oversees what happens on earth and will punish the wicked for their behavior. The psalmist has received from the Lord the strength of a wild bull ready for combat (v. 11a). The rich oil (v. 11b) suggests both virility and health.

The psalmist sharply contrasts the fate of the wicked and the just. The "wicked flourish like grass" (v. 8), sprouting green herbage after the rain only to perish quickly. The just, however, thrive like the date palm and the towering cedars of Lebanon (v. 13). The wicked are senseless and fools (v. 7) in rejecting true wisdom and the life it calls for. However, the just are perceptive (v. 12), observing the flight of the attackers and their panicky retreat. The future of the wicked contains only "eternal destruction" (v. 8). On the other hand, the future of the just is one of fertility and vigor. "Planted in the house of the LORD" (v. 14a), they enjoy the life and productivity associated with the temple as the source of vitality (see Ezek 47:1-12). Even in their old age, the just will be like trees full of sap (v. 15). The contrast between the two justifies the final remark that the Lord is indeed just (v. 16).

At prayer the lack of specificity of this psalm is an advantage, not a disadvantage. We are thus permitted to reflect on a variety of situations where we suffered unjustly but then experienced reversal because of the One on high (v. 9). We can recall the exuberance of the occasion as we beckoned to others to share in our contagious joy. This recollection is not a trip down nostalgia lane but the precedent for our God's action in the future.

Furthermore, we cannot help but notice the plight of our sisters and brothers who are not yet "[p]lanted in the house of the LORD" (v. 14), perhaps because of injustice. Thus Psalm 92 is a call to action. We are urged to become movers and shakers, so that the "enemy" will not have the upper hand. We are to provide the wherewithal so that our sisters and brothers can ultimately "shout for joy" (v. 5).

## Psalm 118
## Hymn of Thanksgiving

I

¹Give thanks to the LORD, for he is good,
    his mercy endures forever.
²Let Israel say:
    his mercy endures forever.
³Let the house of Aaron say,
    his mercy endures forever.
⁴Let those who fear the LORD say,
    his mercy endures forever.

II

⁵In danger I called on the LORD;
    the LORD answered me and set me free.
⁶The LORD is with me; I am not afraid;
    what can mortals do against me?
⁷The LORD is with me as my helper;
    I shall look in triumph on my foes.
⁸Better to take refuge in the LORD
    than to put one's trust in mortals.
⁹Better to take refuge in the LORD
    than to put one's trust in princes.

III

<sup>10</sup>All the nations surrounded me;
 in the LORD's name I cut them off.
<sup>11</sup>They surrounded me on every side;
 in the LORD's name I cut them off.
<sup>12</sup>They surrounded me like bees;
 they burned up like fire among thorns;
 in the LORD's name I cut them off.
<sup>13</sup>I was hard pressed and falling,
 but the LORD came to my help.
<sup>14</sup>The LORD, my strength and might,
 has become my savior.

IV

<sup>15</sup>The joyful shout of deliverance
 is heard in the tents of the righteous:
"The LORD's right hand works valiantly;
 <sup>16</sup>the LORD's right hand is raised;
 the LORD's right hand works valiantly."
<sup>17</sup>I shall not die but live
 and declare the deeds of the LORD.
<sup>18</sup>The LORD chastised me harshly,
 but did not hand me over to death.

V

<sup>19</sup>Open the gates of righteousness;
 I will enter and thank the LORD.
<sup>20</sup>This is the LORD's own gate,
 through it the righteous enter.
<sup>21</sup>I thank you for you answered me;
 you have been my savior.
<sup>22</sup>The stone the builders rejected
 has become the cornerstone.
<sup>23</sup>By the LORD has this been done;
 it is wonderful in our eyes.
<sup>24</sup>This is the day the LORD has made;
 let us rejoice in it and be glad.
<sup>25</sup>LORD, grant salvation!
 LORD, grant good fortune!

VI

²⁶Blessed is he
   who comes in the name of the LORD.
We bless you from the house of the LORD.
   ²⁷The LORD is God and has enlightened us.
Join in procession with leafy branches
   up to the horns of the altar.

VII

²⁸You are my God, I give you thanks;
   my God, I offer you praise.
²⁹Give thanks to the LORD, for he is good,
   his mercy endures forever.

The "I" of this psalm is often identified as a king who has experienced social upheaval or some form of political unrest. Having overcome the problem through the Lord's gracious intervention, he sings of this newness in a thanksgiving or psalm of declarative praise. The guests invited to this liturgy of thanksgiving are the whole congregation of Israel and more. The psalm may be divided as follows: (1) opening invitation to liturgical praise (vv. 1-4); (2) thanksgiving song of the king (vv. 5-21); (3) liturgical dialogue involving the king, the priests, and the people (vv. 22-29).

The deliverance of the king is not a private affair since the nation's well-being is tied to his person. In the opening invitation the psalmist sings of the Lord's sense of covenant commitment (v. 1: "good" and "mercy") and then calls on the congregation to join in celebrating the Lord's graciousness to the king. The Israelites (v. 2), the priests (v. 3), and the proselytes (Gentiles who believed in the Lord but did not accept circumcision and the Jewish dietary laws = "those who fear the LORD" [v. 4]) announce that the Lord is indeed a faithful and loyal God. In verses 5-9 the poet begins to describe his former state of disorientation. He cried out in his peril and the Lord responded (v. 5). To experience the Lord's presence is to be able to vanquish any human obstacles (vv. 6-7). To resort to the Lord is far better than to place confidence in mere humans.

In verses 10-14 the psalmist recites the king's account of the danger that made it imperative for him to cry out. The danger is associated with all the nations (v. 10), those cosmic powers that are ever anxious to upset harmony and balance in the world. They were like bees and fire among thorns but they did not win the day owing to the Lord's name (his person) (v. 12). When the king's strength was failing, the Lord stepped in. Salvation means the Lord's faithful response in the face of seemingly insuperable odds (vv. 13-14).

The king's escape is now the occasion for the people's exultation. They take up the song of the Lord's victorious right hand (vv. 15-16). Actually, they are celebrating more than an isolated case of divine intervention. When death threatened the king, their own world was threatened with upheaval and disruption (vv. 17-18). Death is an apt term for the state of disorientation. In verse 19 the king asks to enter the sanctuary since he has experienced the Lord's righteousness. After the priest's affirmative answer in verse 20, the king formally proclaims the message of newness in verse 21: "I thank you for you answered me; / you have been my savior."

In verses 22-25 the people articulate their sense of bewilderment and amazement. The stone rejected by the builders has become nothing less than the cornerstone (v. 22). This is indeed a world of radical reversals—only the Lord can be responsible for this surprising turn of events (v. 23). It is the appropriate time for celebration and hence for further requests for deliverance (vv. 24-25).

As the liturgical dialogue continues, the priests now pronounce a blessing over both the king and the assembly and bid them to approach to the very horns of the altar (vv. 26-27) and to participate in the sacrifice. Fittingly the king addresses his message of praise to the Lord once more (v. 28). In keeping with the introduction of the psalm, it is a message that the people are to proclaim as well (v. 29). Goodness is always a treasure to be shared with others.

At prayer we must make God's gift-giving our own contagious experience. Like the people in Psalm 118, we are to be touched by God's graciousness to others. Whenever disease, hatred, unemployment, loneliness, and despair give way to health, love, jobs, community, and hope, we must join in the chorus. What were once construction rejects are now an edifying testimony to a concerned God (v. 22) who likes to surprise us, assuring us that despite rumors to the contrary he is alive and well.

We humans find it relatively easy to praise our God's surprising gifts. It is the graciousness of others that is difficult to acknowledge. Yet at prayer we can find a God who bewilders and amazes us with his gifted servants who make possible the trek to reorientation for others. They are so often the unassuming people who visit nursing homes, who provide for the homeless, who console the bereaved, and so on. Wherever they are, "Amazing Grace" is present. Prayer is the fitting moment to confess that presence and to sing of a God who seldom chooses to effect his surprises completely alone.

Psalm 118 is a challenge to our prayer life in another way. It makes us aware of the rejects in our own life (v. 22). They are the living dead (vv. 17-18), the mute monuments to our inhumanity. Prayer is the call to a liturgy of rehabilitation whereby the rejects can recover their self-esteem and thereby reflect a God of surprises. Our eucharistic prayer especially is that dangerous place where we promise to be food and drink for others. Eucharist is the prayer that pulls together the pain of rejection and the thrill of transformation in the passion-death-resurrection of Jesus. To approach the altar (v. 27) means to leave the sanctuary in search of the rejects. Eucharist is to be the stimulus for radical gift-giving.

## Psalm 103
### Praise of Divine Goodness

¹Of David.

I

Bless the LORD, my soul;
    all my being, bless his holy name!
²Bless the LORD, my soul;
    and do not forget all his gifts,
³Who pardons all your sins,
    and heals all your ills,
⁴Who redeems your life from the pit,
    and crowns you with mercy and compassion,
⁵Who fills your days with good things,
    so your youth is renewed like the eagle's.

II

⁶The LORD does righteous deeds,
    brings justice to all the oppressed.
⁷He made known his ways to Moses,
    to the Israelites his deeds.

⁸Merciful and gracious is the LORD,
    slow to anger, abounding in mercy.
⁹He will not always accuse,
    and nurses no lasting anger;
¹⁰He has not dealt with us as our sins merit,
    nor requited us as our wrongs deserve.

III

¹¹For as the heavens tower over the earth,
    so his mercy towers over those who fear him.
¹²As far as the east is from the west,
    so far has he removed our sins from us.
¹³As a father has compassion on his children,
    so the LORD has compassion on those who fear him.
¹⁴For he knows how we are formed,
    remembers that we are dust.
¹⁵As for man, his days are like the grass;
    he blossoms like a flower in the field.
¹⁶A wind sweeps over it and it is gone;
    its place knows it no more.
¹⁷But the LORD's mercy is from age to age,
    toward those who fear him.
His salvation is for the children's children
    ¹⁸of those who keep his covenant,
    and remember to carry out his precepts.

IV

¹⁹The LORD has set his throne in heaven;
    his dominion extends over all.
²⁰Bless the LORD, all you his angels,
    mighty in strength, acting at his behest,
    obedient to his command.
²¹Bless the LORD, all you his hosts,
    his ministers who carry out his will.
²²Bless the LORD, all his creatures,
    everywhere in his domain.
    Bless the LORD, my soul!


Although some consider Psalm 103 a psalm of descriptive praise because of such passages as verses 1-2 and 19-21, there is good reason

for regarding it as a thanksgiving or psalm of declarative praise. The psalmist experienced God's healing after a serious illness. In praising God for this miraculous deliverance, he links his personal experience with the experience of Israel. The psalm may be divided as follows: (1) introduction (vv. 1-2); (2) thanksgiving for healing on the part of the psalmist (vv. 3-5); (3) thanksgiving for the Lord's abiding fidelity and concern on the part of Israel (vv. 6-18); (4) conclusion (vv. 19-22).

In the introduction (vv. 1-2) the self ("my soul") summons the self to praise the Lord. A key phrase here is "all his gifts" (v. 2). The rest of the psalm will be a recital of those gifts that both the psalmist and Israel as a whole have received. In the second section (vv. 3-5) the author establishes a link between his sinfulness and his illness (v. 4). (This is not an uncommon connection—see Ps 107:17; John 9:2; Jas 5:14-16.) What is central to the experience of restoration to health is God's love ("mercy") and compassion (v. 4), a theme that the psalmist will exploit in the third section. A vivid image of this recovery is that of the psalmist's youth being "renewed like the eagle's" (v. 5). This is probably a reference to the eagle as a symbol of vitality (see Isa 40:31).

In the third section the psalmist incorporates Israel's similar experience of divine compassion and care: mercy and grace (v. 8), love (v. 11: "mercy"), compassion (v. 13), kindness/mercy (v. 17). In verse 7 the author focuses on Israel's deliverance in the exodus. There the Lord demonstrated the mercy and graciousness of a mother (v. 8; see Exod 34:6-7; Ps 145:8). In verses 9-12 the psalmist develops the Lord's fidelity in dealing with Israel's guilt. In verses 13-18 he heightens this sense of covenant love by commenting on human frailty and mortality. In the Lord's handling of both Israel's guilt and human frailty, the author notes that the divine actions are not like anything Israel expects. This God does not dispense equal punishment for human sinfulness (v. 10). This God does not let his anger burn forever (v. 9). Indeed the Lord's compassion and forgiveness far surpass human expectations and calculations. Besides being a mother (v. 8), this God is also a father who cannot restrain his compassion for his children (v. 13). One would be a fool to attempt to measure God's capacity to give.

In the conclusion (vv. 19-22) the psalmist's huge audience of those offering praise to the Lord includes the angels (v. 20), the hosts of heaven (v. 21), and all earth-creatures (v. 22). In this mighty chorus the psalmist includes himself. The end of the psalm is exactly like the beginning: the self summons the self to praise the Lord.

At prayer we must consider our tendency to place limits on God's gift-giving. We feel that God should act proportionately. His generosity and compassion must be restrained. In so thinking, we fashion this God in our own image. We are unwilling to let God be God and thus give disproportionately. In effect we are latter-day Jonahs. We do not want the Lord to show any mercy to our modern-day inhabitants of Nineveh (see Jonah 4:1-11). We want effective control of the Lord's capacity to give. Psalm 103 is a healthy reminder that we are all too human. We must learn that this God is a God of surprises who will not brook any human effort to curtail his compassion and concern.

Psalm 103 is an instructive reminder of the link between the individual and the community, namely, the bond between the psalmist and Israel. We are urged to see God's generosity to us as individuals within the context of community. Thus the God who delivers and reorients us is the God who delivers and reorients the community. We must use our personal experiences to give hope to others. We should feel compelled to bring our reversals before the community so that they may rejoice with us (see Luke 15:4-10). At prayer we must realize that we bring these graces to the notice of the community so that they too may thus begin the trek from sickness to health, from disorientation to reorientation.

## Psalm 116
### Thanksgiving to God Who Saves from Death

I
¹I love the LORD, who listened
    to my voice in supplication,
²Who turned an ear to me
    on the day I called.
³I was caught by the cords of death;
    the snares of Sheol had seized me;
    I felt agony and dread.
⁴Then I called on the name of the LORD,
    "O LORD, save my life!"

II

⁵Gracious is the LORD and righteous;
    yes, our God is merciful.
⁶The LORD protects the simple;
    I was helpless, but he saved me.
⁷Return, my soul, to your rest;
    the LORD has been very good to you.
⁸For my soul has been freed from death,
    my eyes from tears, my feet from stumbling.
⁹I shall walk before the LORD
    in the land of the living.

III

¹⁰I kept faith, even when I said,
    "I am greatly afflicted!"
¹¹I said in my alarm,
    "All men are liars!"
¹²How can I repay the LORD
    for all the great good done for me?
¹³I will raise the cup of salvation
    and call on the name of the LORD.
¹⁴I will pay my vows to the LORD
    in the presence of all his people.
¹⁵Dear in the eyes of the LORD
    is the death of his devoted.
¹⁶LORD, I am your servant,
    your servant, the child of your maidservant;
    you have loosed my bonds.
¹⁷I will offer a sacrifice of praise
    and call on the name of the LORD.
¹⁸I will pay my vows to the LORD
    in the presence of all his people,
¹⁹In the courts of the house of the LORD,
    in your midst, O Jerusalem.
Hallelujah!

This psalm was probably composed for recitation at a liturgy of thanksgiving in the temple precincts. Though it consists mainly of testimony by the psalmist, it does contain direct praise of God (see vv. 16-17).

The likely background is a serious illness (vv. 3, 8, 15) that led to some form of isolation and persecution (v. 11). In its present form the psalm is somewhat indefinite, which allows it to cover more than one situation. It may be divided as follows: (1) the psalmist's distress (vv. 1-4); (2) the Lord's deliverance (vv. 5-9); (3) the psalmist's faith and his vows (vv. 10-14); (4) the psalmist's loyalty and vows (vv. 15-19).

In the first section (vv. 1-4) the psalmist begins by declaring his love and commitment to the Lord (v. 1), who chose to listen to him at the time of his trouble (v. 2). The psalmist then describes his sickness in terms of "the cords of death" and "the snares of Sheol." These images personify both death and serious danger and thus capture the seriousness of the psalmist's situation (see Ps 18:6). Taking up the focus of verse 2, the psalmist acknowledges that salvation resides in God's name (v. 4).

In the second section (vv. 5-9) the poet exploits the dimension of the Lord's covenant loyalty (v. 5: "Gracious" and "merciful"—see Ps 103). "[T]he simple" (v. 6) refers to those who are too vulnerable, too uncomplicated for their own good. In verse 7 the psalmist speaks to himself, assuring himself of security and new peace of mind ("rest"— see Ruth 1:9; 1 Chr 22:9). "[T]he land of the living" (v. 9) is Jerusalem (see Pss 27:13; 52:7). This implies that the psalmist is actually present in the temple (see v. 19).

In the third section (vv. 10-14) the psalmist declares that in the days of his despair he did not lose faith (v. 10), even though he was all too conscious of human infidelity (v. 11). He acknowledges that because of the Lord's utter graciousness, no gift will ever be adequate (v. 12). After all, how does one repay God's overwhelming goodness? Nonetheless he is determined to "raise the cup of salvation" (v. 13). It is likely that this refers to a libation of wine that forms part of the ritual of thanksgiving (see Num 28:7). By this ritual he publicly announces his intention to fulfill the vows he made during the time of his disorientation (v. 14).

In the final section (vv. 15-19) the psalmist declares that the Lord is unwilling to countenance the premature death of one of his faithful ones (vv. 15-16). Because the Lord loosed his bonds, it is only fitting that he acknowledge this indebtedness within the confines of the temple (vv. 17-19). To be sure, this is no burden for the psalmist. He most willingly carries out what he earlier promised.

The whole public nature of the psalmist's thanksgiving may give us pause at prayer to reflect on the Eucharist. Eucharist is that splendid opportunity to fuse together our own personal experience and that of Jesus in the movement from disorientation to reorientation. Using the language of Psalm 116, we too confess that we no longer shed tears of pain, that we no longer stumble about (v. 8). God's graciousness has effected this unimagined reversal. Using the language of Psalm 116 again, we recall that the Father has freed Jesus from "the cords of death" and "the snares of Sheol" (v. 3) by the resurrection. God's fidelity to his Son has effected this unanticipated reversal. In bringing both experiences together in the setting of Eucharist, we indeed "raise the cup of salvation / and call on the name of the LORD" (v. 13). Eucharist is indeed thanksgiving par excellence.

Within our community there are those who still cry, who still stumble, who still are victims of human caprice and treachery. Against the background of Eucharist we are urged to become their agents of resurrection. He who was raised on the third day has sisters and brothers who need resurrection each day. In dismantling the cords and snares that entrap them, we make the transformation of Jesus both the stimulus and reason for the reorientation of our sisters and brothers. Eucharist makes Easter a daily obligation for those who believe in the fullness of the empty tomb.

## Psalm 138
## Hymn of a Grateful Heart

¹Of David.

I

I thank you, Lord, with all my heart;
    in the presence of the angels to you I sing.
²I bow low toward your holy temple;
    I praise your name for your mercy and faithfulness.
For you have exalted over all
    your name and your promise.
³On the day I cried out, you answered;
    you strengthened my spirit.

II

⁴All the kings of earth will praise you, LORD,
    when they hear the words of your mouth.

⁵They will sing of the ways of the LORD:
    "How great is the glory of the LORD!"
⁶The LORD is on high, but cares for the lowly
    and knows the proud from afar.
⁷Though I walk in the midst of dangers,
    you guard my life when my enemies rage.
You stretch out your hand;
    your right hand saves me.
⁸The LORD is with me to the end.
    LORD, your mercy endures forever.
    Never forsake the work of your hands!

While the specific situation of the psalmist is somewhat vague (see v. 3), what makes this thanksgiving somewhat unique is the expansion of the audience. Praise of God is not limited to humans on earth. Those in heaven are also summoned to acknowledge the Lord. Significantly, what binds this whole enterprise of praise together is the Lord's faithful love (vv. 2, 8: "mercy"). The psalm may be divided as follows: (1) thanksgiving for God's intervention (vv. 1-3); (2) the kings' acknowledgment of the Lord's greatness (vv. 4-6); (3) concluding statement of confidence (vv. 7-8).

In the first section (vv. 1-3) the psalmist begins with a fourfold expression of honoring the Lord: thank, sing, bow low, and praise (vv. 1-2). The angels mentioned in verse 1 (literally, "gods") are heavenly beings subordinate to God (see Ps 82:1). These gods have witnesses who attest to their accomplishments (see Isa 41:23; 44:8). It seems that these gods must testify to the Lord's fidelity and love ("mercy") since the God of Israel is exalted over all. However, the Lord's fidelity and love are not vague notions. They become concrete in alleviating the plight of the psalmist (v. 3).

In the second section (vv. 4-6) the scene switches from the heavenly court to earth. The kings of the earth now join the members of that court in confessing the glory of the Lord (vv. 4-5). "Glory" (v. 5), that is, all the trappings of royalty, is what the kings must acknowledge. But the Lord's royal conduct is surprising. It is nothing short of caring for the lowly (v. 6). And this is what the kings must notice. The Lord who is exalted on high is ever attentive to the needs of those who suffer from the shocks and cruelties of life (see Ps 113:5-9).

In the third section (vv. 7-8) the psalmist bases Israel's hope for deliverance not on some vague hypothesis, but on his own personal experience. God guards the life of the psalmist, stretches out his hand over him, and saves him with his right hand (v. 7). The great work of God's hands (v. 8) is the lowly person who can rely solely on the Lord's capacity to turn things dramatically around.

When we experience disorientation, we often succumb to the fallacy that God is not really interested in our problems and concerns. We may feel that we are not persons, only numbers in a vast universe. At prayer we must learn that according to this psalm the Lord who is exalted on high is keenly aware of our predicaments down here on earth. Psalm 138 is proof positive that the Lord shatters the distance between heaven and earth to make his covenant involvement felt. Whenever we experience reorientation, we encounter a very personal God taking a keen interest in our very personal and concrete needs.

At prayer we must also realize that we are part of a huge chorus of praise whenever there is an unexpected reversal. When our sisters and brothers are restored, we must break out into a praise that reverberates throughout the universe. We join hands with the population of heaven and earth in declaring the concrete goodness of our God. We are reminded of the praise of the Risen Lord that Paul taught us so well: "[A]t the name of Jesus / every knee should bend, / of those in heaven and on earth and under the earth, / and every tongue confess that / Jesus Christ is Lord, / to the glory of God the Father" (Phil 2:10-11).

## Psalm 124
## God, the Rescuer of the People

¹A song of ascents. Of David.
Had not the LORD been with us,
    let Israel say,
²Had not the LORD been with us,
    when people rose against us,
³Then they would have swallowed us alive,
    for their fury blazed against us.
⁴Then the waters would have engulfed us,
    the torrent overwhelmed us;
        ⁵then seething water would have drowned us.

⁶Blessed is the LORD, who did not leave us
    to be torn by their teeth.
⁷We escaped with our lives like a bird
    from the fowler's snare;
    the snare was broken,
    and we escaped.
⁸Our help is in the name of the LORD,
    the maker of heaven and earth.

This communal thanksgiving or psalm of declarative praise offers no precise clues as to its setting. Therefore, it refers to no specific national emergency such as the fall of Jerusalem. However, it clearly has in mind some great debacle from which the Lord delivered the community. This psalm appears to be a first reaction to some violent upheaval that leaves the community trembling. Yet this trembling itself attests to the fact that life does go on. It is precisely in this experience that God's involvement is revealed. Hence it is an intense religious experience that acknowledges God's limitless self-giving. At the conclusion of the psalm the agitation dies down, giving way to a statement of exclusive confidence in the Lord. The psalm may be divided as follows: (1) reflections on the national emergency (vv. 1-5); (2) the Lord's deliverance (vv. 6-7); (3) praise of the Creator's intervention (v. 8).

The imagery of disorientation begins with the mention of humans rising up against the community (v. 2). The psalmist then develops the peril by what may be an allusion to the battle against the powers of chaos and the primeval flood. (See Gen 1:2: "and the earth was without form or shape, with darkness over the abyss and a mighty wind sweeping over the waters.") In verse 3 the adversaries are depicted as sea-monsters who in their fury are anxious to swallow up the Lord's people. In verses 4-5 the enemies are raging waters, like the primeval flood, that threaten to inundate the community. For the psalmist the danger is eminently real.

The imagery of liberation or reorientation is found in verses 6-7. The people are not left as prey to the enemies' ravenous teeth. They enjoy the sense of freedom that a bird experiences in escaping from the fowler's snare. The breaking of the snare is the break for freedom.

Verse 8 brings together creation, the divine name, and the experience of deliverance. The Creator, bearing a personal name ("the

Lord"), takes a personal interest in this people. Israel's history attests not to a cosmic god of the ancient Near East but to One who became deeply involved in those events that made up the life of Israel. The outcome of this transforming intervention is that God's people can face the future with renewed confidence. Thanksgiving is the only adequate expression of the transformation.

At community prayer we must recall those transforming events when prejudice, oppression, and manipulation (our modern version of the powers of chaos) were significantly overcome. We must celebrate the goodness of those people whose self-giving ways brought about the breaking of the snare (v. 7). Prayer is to be the occasion for our communal acknowledgment of such successes. The truly human community celebrates here and now the great exploits of its members (the flattery of funeral eulogies comes far too late). To recognize now the gifts of our sisters and brothers is to recognize *the* Giver.

At the same time prayer must move our community to set the stage for future expressions of thanksgiving. At prayer we must recognize those chaotic powers that still oppress our sisters and brothers. Prayer means the setting in motion of that vast machinery that will serve to demolish the new sea-monsters. In reacting to the resurgence of chaos, our God chooses to be with the seemingly frail so that the song of thanksgiving may be made possible for countless others. To experience reorientation is to provide reorientation for others. To receive a gift is to give a gift.

## Psalm 107
## God the Savior of Those in Distress

¹"Give thanks to the Lord for he is good,
    his mercy endures forever!"
²Let that be the prayer of the Lord's redeemed,
    those redeemed from the hand of the foe,
³Those gathered from foreign lands,
    from east and west, from north and south.
I
⁴Some had lost their way in a barren desert;
    found no path toward a city to live in.
⁵They were hungry and thirsty;
    their life was ebbing away.

⁶In their distress they cried to the LORD,
  who rescued them in their peril,
⁷Guided them by a direct path
  so they reached a city to live in.
⁸Let them thank the LORD for his mercy,
  such wondrous deeds for the children of Adam.
⁹For he satisfied the thirsty,
  filled the hungry with good things.

II
¹⁰Some lived in darkness and gloom,
  imprisoned in misery and chains.
¹¹Because they rebelled against God's word,
  and scorned the counsel of the Most High,
¹²He humbled their hearts through hardship;
  they stumbled with no one to help.
¹³In their distress they cried to the LORD,
  who saved them in their peril;
¹⁴He brought them forth from darkness and the shadow of death
  and broke their chains asunder.
¹⁵Let them thank the LORD for his mercy,
  such wondrous deeds for the children of Adam.
¹⁶For he broke down the gates of bronze
  and snapped the bars of iron.

III
¹⁷Some fell sick from their wicked ways,
  afflicted because of their sins.
¹⁸They loathed all manner of food;
  they were at the gates of death.
¹⁹In their distress they cried to the LORD,
  who saved them in their peril,
²⁰Sent forth his word to heal them,
  and snatched them from the grave.
²¹Let them thank the LORD for his mercy,
  such wondrous deeds for the children of Adam.
²²Let them offer a sacrifice in thanks,
  recount his works with shouts of joy.

IV

²³Some went off to sea in ships,
  plied their trade on the deep waters.
²⁴They saw the works of the LORD,
  the wonders of God in the deep.
²⁵He commanded and roused a storm wind;
  it tossed the waves on high.
²⁶They rose up to the heavens, sank to the depths;
  their hearts trembled at the danger.
²⁷They reeled, staggered like drunkards;
  their skill was of no avail.
²⁸In their distress they cried to the LORD,
  who brought them out of their peril;
²⁹He hushed the storm to silence,
  the waves of the sea were stilled.
³⁰They rejoiced that the sea grew calm,
  that God brought them to the harbor they longed for.
³¹Let them thank the LORD for his mercy,
  such wondrous deeds for the children of Adam.
³²Let them extol him in the assembly of the people,
  and praise him in the council of the elders.

V

³³God changed rivers into desert,
  springs of water into thirsty ground,
³⁴Fruitful land into a salty waste,
  because of the wickedness of its people.
³⁵He changed the desert into pools of water,
  arid land into springs of water,
³⁶And settled the hungry there;
  they built a city to live in.
³⁷They sowed fields and planted vineyards,
  brought in an abundant harvest.
³⁸God blessed them, and they increased greatly,
  and their livestock did not decrease.
³⁹But he poured out contempt on princes,
  made them wander trackless wastes,
⁴⁰Where they were diminished and brought low
  through misery and cruel oppression.

⁴¹While he released the poor man from affliction,
    and increased their families like flocks.
⁴²The upright saw this and rejoiced;
    all wickedness shut its mouth.
⁴³Whoever is wise will take note of these things,
    and ponder the merciful deeds of the LORD.

This communal thanksgiving or psalm of declarative praise narrates four types of danger, each joined to a double refrain. The first refrain is, "In their distress they cried to the LORD, / who saved [or similar verb] them in their peril" (vv. 13, 19; see vv. 6, 28). The second refrain is, "Let them thank the LORD for his mercy, / such wondrous deeds for the children of Adam" (vv. 8, 15, 21, 31). Sometime later, possibly after the exile, a new section was added (vv. 33-41), reflecting God's saving action in Israel's history. The psalm may be divided as follows: (1) introduction (vv. 1-3); (2) first type of danger: travel by land (the desert—vv. 4-9); (3) second type of danger: imprisonment (vv. 10-16); (4) third type of danger: mortal illness (vv. 17-22); (5) fourth type of danger: travel by sea (vv. 23-32); (6) the Lord's intervention on behalf of Israel, possibly following the exile (vv. 33-41); (7) conclusion (vv. 42-43).

In the introduction the psalmist focuses on the key terms of the Lord's covenant love ("mercy") and redemption of his people (vv. 1-2). "Redemption" connotes God's intervention because of family ties (see Isa 43:1; 51:10). These two terms, therefore, control all of God's actions in the psalm. Verse 3 may reflect the return of God's people from exile (see Isa 43:5-6).

In the first type of danger (vv. 4-9) the psalmist describes people wandering in the desert. Once they cry out for help, the Lord guides them, satisfying their hunger and thirst. Israel's forty-year experience in the desert after the exodus no doubt serves as the inspiration for this danger. In the second type of danger (vv. 10-16) the psalmist replaces the desert wandering with imprisonment that is due to the people's rebellion against God's word (v. 11). Once they repent, the Lord leads them out of their distress, overcoming darkness and the shadow of death as well as the chains of prison life (v. 14). Quite probably Israel's refusal to enter the Promised Land at God's word is the background for this danger (see Num 14:1-12).

In the third type of danger (vv. 17-22) the psalmist paints a picture of mortal illness. Once again there is a link between serious sickness and human sinfulness (v. 17; see Ps 103:3). In answer to the people's appeal God dispatches the word to heal and snatch them from death (v. 20). In the fourth type of danger (vv. 23-32) the psalmist replaces travel by land with travel by sea. It is the Lord himself who rouses a storm wind by his word (v. 25). However, at the people's cry for help God hushes the storm to a murmur and calms the waves (v. 29; see Matt 8:23-27; Mark 4:35-41; Luke 8:22-25).

In verses 33-41 the Lord intervenes because of another grave danger to his people. Part of the biblical background here seems to be the Lord's destruction of the cities of Sodom and Gomorrah (Gen 18–19). Adapting that tradition, the psalmist depicts God overwhelming the inhabitants of the land of Canaan to prepare a way for Israel (vv. 33-34). God then leads them through the desert to a fertile land (vv. 35-38) and defends them from all dangers (vv. 39-41). As mentioned earlier, this section may reflect Israel's return from exile. According to the exilic prophet Second Isaiah the Lord transforms the desert into a well-watered land (the very opposite of vv. 4-9; see Isa 41:17-19; 43:19-20).

According to the conclusion (vv. 42-43) the events in the psalm are far from being devoid of meaning. They are all charged with a sense of God's involvement with humanity that leads the upright to rejoice and the wicked to be silent (v. 42). In the last resort all these scenes are "the merciful deeds of the LORD" (v. 43).

At prayer we can easily profit from the sweep of this beautiful psalm. In place of the four types of danger (vv. 4-32) we can insert our own experiences, such as death of a loved one, breakup of a relationship, addictions of various kinds, unemployment, and so forth. To be sure, these dangers are no less serious than those depicted in Psalm 107. For us they mean life ebbing away (v. 5), darkness and "the shadow of death" (vv. 10, 14), "the gates of death" (v. 18), reeling and staggering like drunkards (v. 27). If God intervened for his people then, will he do less for us now?

The second and third types of danger (vv. 10-16, 17-22) involve sinfulness of one form or another. In disorientation we are often the victims of our sense of devastating guilt. We cannot imagine that our sinfulness can be the point of departure for growth in our relationship with the Lord and our community. Psalm 107 urges us to cry out to the Lord and our community in our pain and distress. Reorientation is the calming of our sea (v. 29), safe conduct through our desert (v. 7), and the dismantling of our chains (v. 14). Covenant empowers us to hope for such transformations.

## New Testament

### Matthew 21:33-43

³³"Hear another parable. There was a landowner who planted a vineyard, put a hedge around it, dug a wine press in it, and built a tower. Then he leased it to tenants and went on a journey. ³⁴When vintage time drew near, he sent his servants to the tenants to obtain his produce. ³⁵But the tenants seized the servants and one they beat, another they killed, and a third they stoned. ³⁶Again he sent other servants, more numerous than the first ones, but they treated them in the same way. ³⁷Finally, he sent his son to them, thinking, 'They will respect my son.' ³⁸But when the tenants saw the son, they said to one another, 'This is the heir. Come, let us kill him and acquire his inheritance.' ³⁹They seized him, threw him out of the vineyard, and killed him. ⁴⁰What will the owner of the vineyard do to those tenants when he comes?" ⁴¹They answered him, "He will put those wretched men to a wretched death and lease his vineyard to other tenants who will give him the produce at the proper times." ⁴²Jesus said to them, "Did you never read in the scriptures:

'The stone that the builders rejected
has become the cornerstone;
by the Lord has this been done,
and it is wonderful in our eyes'?
⁴³Therefore, I say to you, the kingdom of God will be taken away from you and given to a people that will produce its fruit."

It is possible that the original parable of the unjust tenant farmers concluded with verse 39. A landowner did not get his due share of the harvest from his tenant farmers. After two futile attempts (the sending of servants and still more servants), the landowner sent his son. However, taking advantage of the son's status as heir, the tenant farmers murdered him.

Christian tradition added material from Isaiah's song of the vine-yard (a symbol of God's people—see Isa 5:1-7) with the planting of the vineyard (v. 33) and the question (v. 40). Christian tradition also interpreted the son as Jesus. At this point the movement from disori-entation to reorientation becomes central. Since death was not God's last word with regard to his Son's fate, the Christian community went on to speak of his exaltation. Appropriately, the community cited Psalm 118:22-23 (v. 42; see also Acts 4:11; 1 Pet 2:7). Owing to the Father's intervention the rejected stone eventually became the cornerstone. For the Christian community Jesus' original parable of a disconcerting affair in Galilee became a model of disorientation-reorientation: human violence is offset by divine intervention.

At prayer the resurrection of Jesus must be our central model of reorientation. Jesus' resurrection was not resuscitation but transforma-tion. Hence he was on a new level of being. By his willingness to chal-lenge the old securities and thereby accept death he was made capable of a new type of life. At prayer we cannot simply say that the Lord regained everything he had surrendered at the moment of becoming human. That would be to disregard his life, especially as it culminated in passion and death. The Risen Lord attains reorientation only at the cost of disorientation. It is this gift-giving of Jesus that makes possible the gift-giving of the Father. To applaud the Father's gift is to let go of our focus on self and to make Christ the center of our lives. It is this centrality that makes possible new empty tombs and third-day activi-ties. Easter is an essential ingredient of all prayer.

### Luke 15:11-32

[11]Then he said, "A man had two sons, [12]and the younger son said to his father, 'Father, give me the share of your estate that should come to me.' So the father divided the property between them. [13]After a few days, the younger son collected all his belongings and set off to a distant country where he squandered his inheri-tance on a life of dissipation. [14]When he had freely spent every-thing, a severe famine struck that country, and he found himself in dire need. [15]So he hired himself out to one of the local citizens who sent him to his farm to tend the swine. [16]And he longed to eat his fill of the pods on which the swine fed, but nobody gave

him any. [17]Coming to his senses he thought, 'How many of my father's hired workers have more than enough food to eat, but here am I, dying from hunger. [18]I shall get up and go to my father and I shall say to him, "Father, I have sinned against heaven and against you. [19]I no longer deserve to be called your son; treat me as you would treat one of your hired workers."' [20]So he got up and went back to his father. While he was still a long way off, his father caught sight of him, and was filled with compassion. He ran to his son, embraced him and kissed him. [21]His son said to him, 'Father, I have sinned against heaven and against you; I no longer deserve to be called your son.' [22]But his father ordered his servants, 'Quickly bring the finest robe and put it on him; put a ring on his finger and sandals on his feet. [23]Take the fattened calf and slaughter it. Then let us celebrate with a feast, [24]because this son of mine was dead, and has come to life again; he was lost, and has been found.' Then the celebration began. [25]Now the older son had been out in the field and, on his way back, as he neared the house, he heard the sound of music and dancing. [26]He called one of the servants and asked what this might mean. [27]The servant said to him, 'Your brother has returned and your father has slaughtered the fattened calf because he has him back safe and sound.' [28]He became angry, and when he refused to enter the house, his father came out and pleaded with him. [29]He said to his father in reply, 'Look, all these years I served you and not once did I disobey your orders; yet you never gave me even a young goat to feast on with my friends. [30]But when your son returns who swallowed up your property with prostitutes, for him you slaughter the fattened calf.' [31]He said to him, 'My son, you are here with me always; everything I have is yours. [32]But now we must celebrate and rejoice, because your brother was dead and has come to life again; he was lost and has been found.'"

Taken merely by itself, this parable falls into two parts: (1) the departure and return of the younger son (vv. 11-24) and (2) the protest of the older son (vv. 25-32). Both parts end with the same saying: "celebrate," "dead/come to life again," and "lost/found." Jesus challenges his audience to imagine the inconsistency of the renegade son at the father's party and the obedient son refusing to join the party. Thus at the end we have a prodigal son inside celebrating and a submissive son outside pouting.

Prior to this parable Luke presents an introduction (15:1-2) and the parables of the lost sheep (15:3-7) and the lost coin (15:8-10). In this setting Jesus is one who receives sinners in God's name simply because they are lost (sheep, coin, son). On the other hand, the Pharisees and scribes (15:2), who complain that Jesus welcomes sinners and eats with them, are in effect the older brother. For them Jesus' gift-giving is out of the question; one must follow the ironclad law of sin and punishment. These Pharisees and scribes are not party people.

At prayer we must be party people. We must candidly confess that our world is overpopulated with older sons who choose to remain outside pouting. We must celebrate the reversals that occur in our lives and the lives of our sisters and brothers. Once we hear the disorientation-reorientation in "dead/come to life again" and "lost/found," we must immediately add "celebrate." Prayer is to be an experience whereby good news becomes contagious, urging on our message of joy and congratulations. To be such partygoers is to express our belief in a God who still performs miracles, especially for those who are seemingly insignificant (one sheep out of a hundred, one coin out of ten, one prodigal son versus an obedient one). Ours is a God who refuses to abide by our carefully enacted rules. Hence the transformation of a prodigal means prodigal celebration on the part of all, not the pouting of supposedly correct and obedient children. To pray the thanksgiving or psalm of declarative praise is ultimately to prepare for the banquet that is the fulfillment of the kingdom of God (see Matt 8:11). Only partygoers are permitted.

## Summary of the theology of the psalms of declarative praise

1. We are challenged to reject our distaste for "newness." We are urged to admit a God of surprises.
2. We are invited to imitate our God in the transformation of pain into joy. We are called upon to effect surprises for others because we believe in a God of surprises.
3. We are encouraged to see our gifts as gifts for others. It is these gifts that can counteract the inhumanity of our world and thus bring about reorientation.

4. We are asked to observe the goodness of others and to label it "good, very good" (Gen 1:10-31). Our God continues to surprise us in and through others.

5. We are compelled to rediscover our sense of celebration. In Eucharist we are to share the burdens of others by sharing the bread and the wine. To celebrate Eucharist is to restore our God's capacity to give and effect surprises.

# Suggestions for Further Study

## Commentaries

Allen, Leslie C. *Psalms 101–150*. Revised ed. Word Biblical Commentary. Nashville: Nelson, 2002.

Alter, Robert. *The Book of Psalms*. New York: W. W. Norton, 2007.

Brueggemann, Walter. *The Message of the Psalms: A Theological Commentary*. Augsburg Old Testament Studies. Minneapolis: Augsburg, 1984.

Craigie, Peter C. *Psalms 1–50*. Word Biblical Commentary. Nashville: Nelson, 1983.

Davidson, Robert. *The Vitality of Worship: A Commentary on the Book of Psalms*. Grand Rapids: Eerdmans, 1998.

Gerstenberger, Erhard S. *Psalms: Part 1, with an Introduction to Cultic Poetry*. Forms of Old Testament Literature. Grand Rapids: Eerdmans, 1988.

———. *Psalms: Part 2, and Lamentations*. Forms of Old Testament Literature. Grand Rapids: Eerdmans, 2001.

Goldingay, John. *Psalms*. Baker Commentary on the Old Testament Wisdom and Psalms. 3 vols. Grand Rapids: Baker, 2006–2008.

Hossfeld, Frank Lothar, and Erich Zenger. *Psalms 2: A Commentary on Psalms 51–100*. Hermeneia. Minneapolis: Fortress, 2005.

———. *Psalms 3: A Commentary on Psalms 101–150*. Hermeneia. Minneapolis: Fortress, 2011.

Kraus, Hans-Joachim. *Psalms 1–59*. Continental Commentary. Minneapolis: Augsburg, 1988.

———. *Psalms 60–150*. Continental Commentary. Minneapolis: Augsburg, 1989.

Mays, James L. *Psalms*. Interpretation. Louisville: John Knox, 1994.

Stuhlmueller, Carroll. *Psalms*. Old Testament Message. 2 vols. Wilmington: Michael Glazier, 1983.

Tate, Marvin E. *Psalms 51–100*. Word Biblical Commentary. Dallas: Word, 1990.

Terrien, Samuel. *The Psalms: Strophic Structure and Theological Commentary.* Grand Rapids: Eerdmans, 2003.

Weiser, Artur. *The Psalms*. Old Testament Library. Philadelphia: Westminster, 1962.

Westermann, Claus. *The Living Psalms*. Grand Rapids: Eerdmans, 1989.

## Other Studies

Alonso Schökel, Luis. *Treinta Salmos: Poesía y oración*. Estudios de Antiguo Testamento. Madrid: Cristiandad, 1981.

Anderson, Bernhard W. *Out of the Depths: The Psalms Speak for Us Today.* 3rd revised and expanded ed. Louisville: Westminster John Knox, 2000.

Bellinger, W. H., Jr. *Psalms: Reading and Studying the Book of Praises*. Peabody: Hendrickson, 1990.

Brown, William P. *Seeing the Psalms: A Theology of Metaphor*. Louisville: Westminster John Knox, 2002.

Brueggemann, Walter. *Praying the Psalms: Engaging Scripture and the Life of the Spirit*. 2nd ed. Eugene, OR: Cascade, 2007.

———. *Israel's Praise: Doxology against Idolatry and Ideology*. Philadelphia: Fortress, 1988.

———. *Abiding Astonishment: Psalms, Modernity, and the Making of History.* Literary Currents in Biblical Interpretation. Louisville: Westminster John Knox, 1991.

———. *The Psalms and the Life of Faith*. Edited by Patrick D. Miller. Minneapolis: Fortress, 1995.

Dunlop, Laurence. *Patterns of Prayer in the Psalms*. New York: Seabury, 1992.

Endres, John C., and Elizabeth Liebert. *A Retreat with the Psalms: Resources for Personal and Communal Prayer*. New York: Paulist, 2001.

Gunkel, Hermann, and Joachim Begrich. *An Introduction to the Psalms: The Genres of the Religious Lyric of Israel*. Mercer Library of Biblical Studies. Macon, GA: Mercer University Press, 1998.

Guthrie, Harvey H. *Israel's Sacred Songs: A Study of Dominant Themes*. New York: Seabury, 1966.

———. *Theology as Thanksgiving: From Israel's Psalms to the Church's Eucharist*. New York: Seabury, 1981.

Harrington, Daniel J. *Why Do We Hope? Images in the Psalms*. Collegeville, MN: Liturgical Press, 2008.

Holladay, William L. *The Psalms through Three Thousand Years: Prayerbook of a Cloud of Witnesses*. Minneapolis: Fortress, 1993.

Keel, Othmar. *The Symbolism of the Ancient World: Ancient Near Eastern Iconography and the Book of Psalms.* Winona Lake, IN: Eisenbrauns, 1997.

Kraus, Hans-Joachim. *Theology of the Psalms.* Continental Commentary. Minneapolis: Augsburg, 1986.

Mays, James L. *The Lord Reigns: A Theological Handbook to the Psalms.* Louisville: Westminster John Knox, 1994.

McCann, J. Clinton, Jr. *A Theological Introduction to the Psalms: The Psalms as Torah.* Nashville: Abingdon, 1993.

Miller, Patrick D., Jr. *Interpreting the Psalms.* Philadelphia: Fortress, 1986.

———. *They Cried to the Lord: The Form and Theology of Biblical Prayer.* Minneapolis: Fortress, 1994.

Mowinckel, Sigmund. *The Psalms in Israel's Worship.* Reprint (2 vols. in 1). Sheffield: JSOT, 1991.

Murphy, Roland E. *The Psalms Are Yours.* New York: Paulist, 1993.

Pleins, J. David. *The Psalms: Songs of Tragedy, Hope, and Justice.* Maryknoll, NY: Orbis, 1993.

Ringgren, Helmer. *The Faith of the Psalmists.* Philadelphia: Fortress, 1963.

Sabourin, Leopold. *The Psalms: Their Origin and Meaning.* 2nd ed. New York: Alba House, 1974.

Seybold, Klaus. *Introducing the Psalms.* Edinburgh: T & T Clark, 1990.

Smith, Mark S. *Psalms: The Divine Journey.* New York: Paulist, 1987.

Stuhlmueller, Carroll. *The Spirituality of the Psalms.* Collegeville, MN: Liturgical Press, 2002.

Wahl, Thomas P. *The Lord's Song in a Foreign Land: The Psalms as Prayer.* Collegeville, MN: Liturgical Press, 1998.

Westermann, Claus. *The Praise of God in the Psalms.* Richmond: John Knox, 1965.

———. *The Psalms: Structure, Content, and Message.* Minneapolis: Augsburg, 1980.

———. *Praise and Lament in the Psalms.* Atlanta: John Knox, 1981.

Wilson, Gerald H. *The Editing of the Hebrew Psalter.* SBL Dissertation Series. Chico, CA: Scholars Press, 1985.

# Index of Biblical Passages